What people are s

Glowing Deeper

The timing was perfect when I read this book. I'd just gone through a devastating loss. I really recommend it; it's an amazing investigation into the Spirit World at a comforting level.
Shannon Sylvia, *My Horror Story*, Apple TV

A wonderful book for anyone seeking understanding of the spirit dimensions of life.
Claire Broad, medium, spiritual teacher, and author

For anybody interested in the paranormal, Spirit Guides, mediumship, even the history of witchcraft, check out *Glowing Deeper*!
Paul Bradford, *Trending Fear*, Discovery Channel; *Ghost Hunters International*, SYFY Channel

Also by this Author

Letting Glow: a guide to intuition, spirituality, and living consciously.
ISBN: 978 1 80341 220 7

Glowing Deeper

Book Two of the Letting Glow Trilogy.

Glowing Deeper

Book Two of the Letting Glow Trilogy.

Phill Webster

BOOKS

Winchester, UK
Washington, USA

JOHN HUNT PUBLISHING

First published by O-Books, 2024
O-Books is an imprint of John Hunt Publishing Ltd., 3 East St., Alresford,
Hampshire SO24 9EE, UK
office@jhpbooks.com
www.johnhuntpublishing.com
www.o-books.com

For distributor details and how to order please visit the 'Ordering' section on our website.

ISBN: 978 1 80341 436 2
978 1 80341 437 9 (ebook)
Library of Congress Control Number: 2022948809

A CIP catalogue record for this book is available from the British Library.

Design: Lapiz Digital Services

UK: Printed and bound by CPI Group (UK) Ltd, Croydon, CR0 4YY
Printed in North America by CPI GPS partners

The author of this book does not dispense medical advice or
prescribe the use of any technique as a form of treatment for
physical, emotional, or medical problems without the advice of a
physician, either directly or indirectly. The intent of the author
is only to offer information of a general nature to help you in
your quest for emotional and spiritual well-being. In the event
you use any of the information in this book for yourself, which is
your constitutional right, the author and the publisher assume no
responsibility for your actions.

We operate a distinctive and ethical publishing philosophy in
all areas of our business, from our global network of authors to
production and worldwide distribution.

Contents

For my mom, Maureen Webster. For everything you did for me, and for every adventure we had. Thank you for still being close. My love forever.

… and to Laura, love of my life and my best friend. Thank you for your unending support and patience.

Special thanks to my teachers, Claire Broad, Gilly Hall, Gordon Smith, James Van Praagh, Puma Quispe Singona, and Manari Ushigua, for your wisdom.

My Guides, for their contribution and truths.

Thank you to Gerard Siles and Taina, for sharing your experiences.

Last but not least, thank you to the team at O-Books for your faith and commitment to these books.

Introduction: Letting Glow

In 2021, I lost my mother. After a year of isolating at home through the COVID-19 pandemic, her soul decided that she'd had enough, and she left the physical world. I was devastated. When we lose a parent, we lose the one true witness to our lives. We lose the person who saw us take our first steps, who heard us speak our first words, who sheltered and nourished us, taught us, and was there for us every single time. I took it hard. I'm still taking it hard, nearly two years on. Grief doesn't simply go away. It is not linear. It shows up every day, a couple of seconds after waking. It follows you through the grocery store. It wakes you up in the middle of the night. It permeates your dreams. It's on the TV, and it's in songs it wasn't part of before. It's out in nature, and welcomes you with each new season. And when you want to get away, it travels with you on holidays.

Your friends will tell you it's time to move on. Friends who haven't crawled on all fours at night, drunk on wine and punching the floor with tears soaking their face. They'll tell you, "It's what they would have wanted," when they didn't even know them. The most caring of friends, who have yet to experience the depths of despair that you are going through, will do or say the wrong thing after a couple of drinks at a party, and you will find yourself biting your tongue in response to the unwitting blow they have just dealt you. After a couple of months, your work colleagues will expect you to be OK again. They don't know about the hollow dark spiral that churns in your chest when you think about those last months, those last conversations, or that day. That day that changed everything.

Grief led me to enlightenment. Because I couldn't cope with the pain. And because I needed to know there was something more. Something beyond the everyday mundane. That there was something to those brief glimpses of the ethereal, and the magic,

1

before the unrelenting, habitual thoughts crept back in again. Grief led me on a spiritual journey, a wild, all-encompassing search to prove that there is more, and that my mom is still out there somewhere, conscious of my life, safe, and that someday we will be reunited.

The day she died, I climbed into her empty bed feeling raw and numb. I don't remember much of the evening other than the desolate sorrow that permeates every thought of that day. I drifted in and out of sleep, my mom's smell on the pillow, the shock of losing her still reverberating through my core as each time I woke up I remembered this terrible alternate reality anew, over and over again.

I stood facing her in a room, a room full of swirling colors and ethereal walls. The colors that decorated them were alive and in motion, and she stood before a door. I was right there. Not distanced or detached like in a regular dream. I was in front of her, holding her hands.

"They said that it was your heart," I told her. She frowned, and one of her hands let go of mine and went instinctively to her chest, touching it lightly.

"Are you going to be alright?" she asked me. I couldn't help but smile. She was always thinking of me before herself, even as she was about to cross the final threshold and transition from this world to the next.

"I'll be fine," I reassured her. "Honestly. You have to go now." I was being smarter than usual. I felt like the smartest version of myself. My best self. My Higher Self. It didn't show up very often. Unselfish and thinking of the greater good. If we'd have been having this conversation at a conscious level I would have never let her go.

"Are you sure?" she asked.

"Mum," I said, a little sternly. "Really, it's time to go. I promise you, it's going to be amazing." I smiled.

I felt her go. I don't remember her turning to leave. I woke up in tears.

The *American Journal of Hospice & Palliative Medicine* writes, "Anecdotal evidence suggests that some loved ones and caregivers of dying patients undergo a type of end-of-life phenomena known as a shared death experience or SDE, whereby one feels that one has participated in a dying person's transition to a post-mortem existence." They conducted a content analysis report of 164 SDEs, revealing four distinct though nonexclusive modes of an SDE: remotely sensing a death from a location far away, witnessing unusual phenomena, such as seeing the dying person's "spirit" leave the body at the moment of death, feelings of accompanying the dying, and feelings of assisting the dying. Analysis also revealed three major domains of SDE effects, resulting in changes in belief, the reconciliation of grief, and the perception of continued relational bonds with the deceased.

This was only part of what I learned in the months that followed my mother's death, about the continued existence of life, after death. I needed more. I asked for signs, and I got them. I got them repeatedly. I started to think about other things that had happened to me in the past. Things that couldn't be rationally explained, and I began to realize there had been many.

I read books. I slowly began to dispel the notion of the supernatural and opened up to the possibility that so-called esoteric events were entirely natural. What if they were real? What if the mystical experiences people talked of, people from all walks of life, were actually a thing? What if it were simply a case of reconnecting with our intuition and changing our frequency to be able to sense subtle energies all around us? We are, after all, becoming less and less in tune with our natural state. We wedge ourselves into overpriced apartments in cities with constant distractions. Technology is moving forward so rapidly that we think less in order to produce more. We've lost touch with nature and we suppress and cultivate our basic instincts. What if moments of inspiration, gut feeling, and ingenuity are the same as intuition, divination, and clairvoyance? What if the so-called "supernatural" is actually "super natural"? I secretly started looking into mediumship. I didn't tell anyone for fear of ridicule, or at best a sympathetic condescendence that I was going through the denial stage of grief. I met with mediums, and they immediately began telling me that *I* would become a medium. I started meditating. I began learning about this thing they all called Spirit, and how to open up to it. Wonderful things began to happen. Not the least of which being a message from my mother, three months after she had passed away, through a medium in a small Spiritualist Church in London. This changed everything. *Everything.* I attended workshops and devoured all I could find on the subject of life after death. I became a member of the London College of Psychic Studies. I took courses, and sat in on Zoom calls with spiritual teachers whose books I'd read. I started attending the Spiritualist Association of Great Britain in Battersea, London. I was invited to join a medium development circle. I began to explore beyond mediumship and studied with Medicine Men and descendants of the indigenous tribes of North and South America, and learned about Sacred Energies. I studied female spirituality in ancient times through the University of Barcelona. I trained to become a Past Life Regression Therapist. My connection with Spirit grew stronger, my awareness expanded, and a new perspective began to form. My world got a little brighter, and I wrote a book called *Letting Glow.*

Throughout the process of writing, it would often seem as though something beyond myself stepped in and wrote parts of the book for me. I know this sounds a little "out there" for some people. And I say this neither to relinquish responsibility for the messages in the book, nor to make it appear more grandiose than it actually is. But the fact was that within days of submitting it to ten or so publishers, I was offered four traditional book deals from four very different publishing houses, and more followed in the months to come from all over the world. I was both humbled and reassured that the messages in the book were destined to be read. My own story was just a vehicle to carry them on. If other people had also experienced glimpses into the unknown, then sharing my own encounters with the esoteric could perhaps help someone make sense of theirs. So as I progress on this journey I would like to invite you along with me. I am still no expert on the subject of the so-called supernatural. I'm certainly no guru. But I have witnessed incredible things over these past two years that have proven to me beyond a shadow of a doubt that what we call the unknown can be known. Mystical experiences are real. So let's get to it.

We'll expand on Book One and revisit some familiar themes, but we shall go deeper. Part One of this book will get straight into the metaphysical. It will pick up where *Letting Glow* left off. It can be a challenging read but it shall build the groundwork to activate our intuition. Part Two will ease up a little and we shall explore themes such as the paranormal, ancient rituals, astral projection and other fun stuff. Part Three will expand our journey towards mediumship. When we get to the exercises and meditations, I invite you to read through them a few times and familiarize yourself with the directions before attempting them. Better still, if you are reading the hard copy of this work, record yourself reading them aloud then play them back as guided meditations. All of them will require the ability to use your imagination and create powerful visualizations in your mind's eye. We are going to explore how to do this in the first few chapters. As tempting as it may be, please try not to skip any exercises, as each will build upon the last, particularly in

Part One. If completing an exercise isn't practically possible (for example if you are reading this on your lunch break, or in the dentist waiting room) then return to them in order at a later date. To get the most from this work, I strongly encourage you to incorporate the messages within these pages in to your daily life. My intuition tells me that my Guides will step in from time to time, usually at the end of a chapter, and the information can be easily identified as it always addresses the greater good. I'm also receiving the impression that I'll finish this book at the end of summer. *The end of your summer* is what specifically comes to mind. I've always considered August 31st the end of summer, ever since I was a kid. I guess it comes from school starting up in September. August 31st is definitely not the last day of summer in the UK, but I tend to mark it as that. We shall see. One thing I am certain of, is that by the end of this book, we shall both know more about the esoteric and Higher Realms than we do right now. Thank you for joining me on this journey. And on a personal note, I want to acknowledge that I couldn't have written this without my mother, Maureen Webster, who through going before me into the next world transformed both of our lives, and brought us all to this book.

Part One: Glowing Within

Chapter One: Intention Is Everything

Before we dive into an exploration of Spirit, we must first lay the foundations for what's to come. Book One finished with the reminder that our limited time on this Earth will unfold regardless of whether we live a life of intent or ignorance. We can choose to take the reins or exist on autopilot. Either way, we will reach our destination. To serve our purpose of spiritual evolution, our intention can help steer us through these unfamiliar waters towards our deeper truth. Before we begin, we must reconnect with our intuition, our soul purpose, and what we envision for our future and choose for our lives. When we are presented with choices, what we seek and aspire to are what guides us, infuses us with meaning, and cuts through the clatter of doubt and distractions that we are relentlessly bombarded with. But it can be difficult to find this internal compass when we get swept up in the daily grind of work, paying bills, family and social obligations, and trying to navigate through each day with minimal discomfort. It's easy to accelerate to a frantic pace before we even realize we're going at breakneck speed. It's equally just as easy to fall into a slumber, to shuffle through life directionless, somnambulist style, drifting from one day to the next in a fog, when our life circumstances have evolved that way. If either of these models ring true with you, then it's time to reconnect with your original intention. It's time to take a moment, find the silence, and tune in. Ask yourself, what is essential to you? What can you not compromise on and what makes you feel alive? When are you at your best? Where are you at your best? Is your environment inspiring your intended outcome? Are your friends encouraging you? What needs to be changed? You *do* know, even if you haven't yet experienced that which you desire. It's like imagining licking something you've never licked before. I know it sounds nuts, but try it. Don't actually start licking random objects, simply imagine doing it. Your tongue knows. Look at any object and imagine licking it. Your brain can produce the feeling in your imagination without you having to actually do it. Your intuition works the same way. It knows. It can be elusive if you haven't used it in awhile. If you've gotten used to letting your thoughts run the show. Don't over question yourself. Don't think: well I'd like to do this but I can't because of that or because of them. Go with your first feeling, before the ifs and buts. You *know*. The you behind the thoughts, the you observing your thoughts. You have the power to set events into motion that can change your circumstances, even if you start small. Change one thing that will point you towards the right direction, and take a little step forward. Take a moment during the day if only for five minutes to close your eyes, concentrate on your breath, and focus. When you begin to notice the distractions creeping in, simply acknowledge them and let them creep on out again. Don't attach any meaning or feeling to them. Let the doubts walk on by, refocus on your breath, and your intended outcome. It really is that simple. What we focus on, we create. All of life works this way. For example, if you think about when you have to get to work on time, you need to plan ahead. You couldn't get there without first visualizing the journey before taking it. You mentally map out what needs to be done before you do it. Even if you do it on autopilot, it still needs to be done. Thoughts are a tool to navigate our way towards our original intention. Use them. Use them to imagine your future. But don't let them take over or turn into doubt and deter you from your purpose. And when your purpose is set, create mantras and say them out loud. There is power in affirmation. Perhaps your soul purpose is to help other people, or to become the person your grandmother believed you to be. Take the steps towards it, navigate forwards with purpose and intention.

"I will help my son through this difficult period in his life."

"By my fiftieth birthday I shall be living in Barbados."

"By the end of the month, I will have completely cut sugar from my diet."

Set the intention in motion by first declaring the intention itself, then take small steps towards it. Tell people about it. Announce your purpose. Write it on social media, or just share it with one best friend. Or don't. If you feel you are already in tune with what you want to do and where you need to be, then quietly get on with it. Keep the affirmations to yourself. The rest will see when the time comes.

Now we're familiar with some of the themes we discussed last time, let's go a step further, and let's go a little deeper.

Chapter Two: Leave a Good Impression

I get the impression. Have you ever used that expression? We've all heard it.

"I get the impression that this job isn't what you expected it to be."

"I have the impression that something positive will come from this situation."

"She didn't leave a good impression."

"I'm impressed."

The Macmillan Dictionary defines the term as "an opinion or feeling that you have about someone or something you have seen but do not know very well". We get the picture, we have a hunch, we pick up, we catch feels, we dig vibes, we cut the air with a knife, and we feel it in our bones. A heightened awareness of our environment, an inner voice, a sense of our surroundings, or not quite putting our finger on it. We have so many ways to describe this elusive, intangible instinct that we often refer to, but when we talk of it as say, I don't know, a sixth sense, all serious discussion goes out of the window and everyone's suddenly looking at you like you landed from Mars. What's so different about instinct, impressions, and love, compared with intuition, ESP, or a feeling of connectedness?

Absolutely nothing.

The examples above show that we all have a sixth sense, and we all have the ability to connect with an inner truth, or our higher selves, the part of us that just *knows* beyond rational thought.

Let's use another comprehensive source. The Oxford Dictionary defines intuition as "the ability to understand something instinctively, without the need for conscious reasoning". We use our intuition all the time, we use it all day long. The trick to developing spiritually is to first recognize intuition as something separate from our thoughts, from the clutter of images and memories bombarding us from morning 'til night and in our sleep. It may be accompanied by a thought; our brains will immediately step in and rationalize the impression as though it were a thought, and then attempt to question it, contradict it, challenge it and dissect it. But we can learn to separate the impression from the thoughts that will jump on it and cling to it like a virus. And the good news is it's pretty easy to do. Are you ready? Halfway through Chapter Two and we're already unlocking the fundamental secrets of mindfulness! Here we go. The impression always comes before the thought. It's that simple. Trust your instincts. Let go. *Use the force.* It's always there, and we've been constantly told about it by our storytellers, our mentors, and our friends. The key is to go with the gut *before* the thoughts rush in. And that may prove tricky to an unfocused mind.

How do you feel? When we go to someone for advice, that's usually the catch-all question that we're presented with. The one that will cut through the crap and expose the truth. But do we really tell them how we feel? Or do we explain every single option our brain has come up with since we encountered the problem we needed advice on? We've spent our whole lives doing that. We're taught to think our way out of any given situation. And don't get me wrong, things do require thought. We couldn't bake a cake by instinct alone. We couldn't set up the new ultra HD television with our feelings. We couldn't learn to drive a car with ESP. And daydreaming and visualizing the future are wonderful things that we need our thoughts for. But in choosing to explore a connection with our higher selves, our consciousness and spirituality, we need to first understand that our sharpest tool is our intuition, or our inner knowing. That which blends with Universal Consciousness.

Book One talked about observing our thoughts, of stepping back and letting them pass on by. We did a visualization exercise called The Mountain and The Mirror, which taught us to first ground ourselves and observe our thoughts with detachment. We are ultimately not our thoughts, we are the ones who look at them. The quiet light inside, always observing, always indifferent. The calm voice in times of crisis, the constant spectator watching the play from the auditorium. The I.

The I that goes to bed with you at night. The I whose heart swells with the sunrise. The I that would weep at the night sky, if the ego would let it. The silent partner in the dual entity that only wants the greater good, beyond desire and conditioning and past traumas and disappointments. That's who we're going to connect with. That's who is behind the facade, and that's who will raise our vibration. I don't mean the ego. I don't mean the personality; I'm talking about the one who is there when you first open your eyes in the morning. In that nanosecond of awareness before the memories crowd in. The one who just before sleep sometimes contemplates the idea that she is aware of herself being aware, and briefly disrupts her own thoughts before they rush back in and bring a welcome complacency. Meditation has been proven to physically alter the brain. In moments of meditation, consciousness is able to observe the brain thinking, and detach itself and recognize itself as both in tune with the physical and the nonphysical, so we can begin to see ourselves as dual entities in a singular unity. Both the observer and the observed, a paradox of physical matter and cosmic energy that is ultimately all one.

So if we are not our thoughts, then what are our thoughts? We're having them, after all. They must be part of us at a physical level. We are having a physical experience as we are clearly biological beings. The brain consists of neurons and their support system, called glial cells. Neurons generate electrical impulses for communication, and we have something close to 100 billion of them. They release chemicals known as neurotransmitters, which generate electrical signals, and these signals propagate like waves, resulting in the formation of thoughts. In the anthropological fields of theology and philosophy, the dichotomy is the belief that we simply consist of a soul and a body. To keep things clear, that is the model we will loosely stick with here since there are a multitude of theories, philosophical meanderings, spiritual insights and indeed scientific facts on the mechanics of the brain and body that could fill up an entire library. I prefer not to muddy the discussion by breaking it down into all of its different sub-cases or talking of non-duality for the time being. We are physical and nonphysical. To use another simplified analysis: we are a soul having a human experience. Now switch that word soul for consciousness, and connect consciousness to a Creator, whoever your chosen Creator might be (God, The Big Bang, Jehovah, The Anunnaki, Flying Spaghetti Monster, whatever) and now we're cooking with gas, as my mom used to say. If we are our consciousness experiencing the physical, listening to our thoughts, sitting quietly and observing, and that consciousness is connected to the All That Is and what we return to after this physical life ends, then we are ultimately the constant, ever-present essence of all existence. We just get so caught up in the daily grind that we forget.

For us to know ourselves as dual entities (physical and nonphysical, we will explore concepts of non-duality at a later date), and to be able to tell the difference between our intuition and our thoughts, we need to recognize our feelings. To lay the foundations for developing at a spiritual level, we need to first begin to know what is intuition and what is conscious reasoning. To be able to go with the first impression rather than getting caught up in the analysis, doubts, and over questioning of the first impression, we need to decipher which is which. It is a subject that we will return to again and again throughout this book. The following exercise will be the groundwork for developing the clarity necessary to explore the esoteric topics we shall get into soon. Familiarize yourself with the text before attempting it, or record yourself reading it out loud and play it back as a guided meditation.

Meditation Exercise: All the Feels. Level: All levels

1. Pay attention to the physical. Concentrating on the breath is an effective tool to focus both the mind and the body. Close your eyes. Focus on the inhale and exhale and relax. Imagine in your mind's eye a clear white cinema screen. The curtains have opened, revealing a blank canvas to project your thoughts onto. Think about a chosen subject (an issue at work, a romantic relationship, a life event), and project it there. Notice any physical sensations that arise in your body. There's no need to change anything, simply sense and observe. Allow sensations to become clear, take shape, and emerge as an emotion or feeling. Recognize this feeling. No need to question it, simply pay attention to your body's reaction when the feeling arises. Perhaps your jaw tightens, perhaps the shoulders tense, perhaps you get butterflies in the stomach. They'll likely be subtle but they'll be there. Notice them, and continue to breathe.

2. Now you have deciphered the body's reaction to the subject, imagine clearing the screen in your mind's eye. The curtains close, and when they reopen, the scene you were projecting there has gone. Pay attention to your feelings, and any subtle changes in your body now that the issue has been temporarily neutralized. They will be

very subtle changes, but they will be recognizable. Do you feel relief? Fear? Sadness? Don't force what you *think* you should feel. Simply observe.

3. Project your situation back onto the screen. Or an entirely different one. Anything you choose. It could be Baby Yoda or your 8th Grade Maths teacher, as long as it elicits a feeling. Hold the image or life event there. Pay attention to the feeling again. Pay attention to any subtle changes in your body. Then after a few moments, close the curtains and wipe that screen clean. Take note of any sensations that arise or disappear with the neutralizing of the subject.

4. Bring your attention back to your breath. While doing so, think on the blank screen and how simple it was to project a life event, and recognize the reactions that accompanied the event. Then think about when you wiped that event from your focus. There was a part of you that took control there, the part of you that closed the curtains and wiped the event away. That part of you was indifferent; after watching from the background, it stepped in and took charge. It wasn't your emotions, it wasn't your physical reactions that you briefly focused on. It was the part of you behind all of the drama you played out, a part of you away from your body's responses, it was the logical knowing that remained detached and simply watched what was going on.

5. Bring yourself back to the present and do something grounding, such as making a cup of tea, going out for a walk, or doing the dishes.

Chapter Three: Child's Play

I have fleeting childhood memories of gliding weightless down the stairs in our home. Bouncing lightly on each step, and floating to the bottom. This memory was amplified when I briefly experienced an ecsomatic event as a teenager, when I purposefully invoked astral travel and felt my consciousness rise above my physical body, as well as my perspective shifting to an impossible angle. This is something we shall delve into later on. But for now I want us to explore the idea that we are perhaps most connected to the spiritual when we are young children. Each new experience is as visceral and real as we will ever feel. The rarest quality of innocence permeates every malleable thought and demand. We have no grasp of an impending death on each of our horizons. We are equally ignorant of economic concerns or carnal desire. Childhood is a time of wonder, of reacting to the world with zero social restrictions placed in our psyche and no inhibitions. We are free to dream and encouraged to conjure and blend our wildest imaginings with the reality we inhabit. We see magic in everything. I remember, in the early 80s, that the adventures of Luke Skywalker were as vital to my day as the food my mom prepared for us to eat. Being able to use my imagination in any way that I chose felt like a secret cheat code to escape an adult world that was beginning to crumble around me. Did everyone know about it? Could we really just quietly drift away and go wherever we wanted in our minds? I would sit staring out the window all day when I started school. I'd wave to my mom going by on the bus to town. Sometimes my dog Lucy would escape from our garden and I'd watch her roam around the playground outside (she'd always be waiting for me at the school gates at the end of the day). My teacher soon put an end to my daydreaming and covered the window next to my seat with other kids' drawings. Slowly but surely, the years go by and innocence makes its way out, while responsibilities work their way in.

Life happens. Before we know it, we're struggling financially, our hearts have been broken a couple of times, we are firmly in the grasp of social constraints, our jobs aren't what we'd hoped for, and the adventures of Luke Skywalker are just something that a giant corporation recycles for endless profit.

I genuinely believe that we had it right back then. We were onto something as kids. I used to say good morning to each tree on the way to school. And I *knew Star Wars* was more important than maths. It still is. I also believe that as children we are more open to esoteric experiences and in tune with all levels of our consciousness. The brain hasn't been conditioned to ignore our inner voice. It doesn't have memories of events to compare experiences to. We simply live in the moment, and we use our thoughts for magic, not misgivings. With this in mind, it makes sense that we would be more in synch with our Higher Selves at an early age, before life creeps in with its various setbacks and rules. Children play. You don't have to tell them to do it, it's completely natural for them. It's something that we move away from as adults, but perhaps there's an art to play that we can still incorporate into our lives. Studies have shown that play is an evolved behavior essential for the well-being of animals. We know this already. We take it for granted that our pets want to play. Think about it. If you have a cat or dog, they're still up for a good play session even as they age. They don't feel embarrassed about it, they love it. They connect with us through it.

At some point during adulthood, a lot of us enjoy revisiting what delighted us as kids. I very recently spoke with an accomplished British celebrity, who writes for the *Observer* as well as authoring five or six books. He told me about his lifelong love for the Belgium comic strip character Tintin. Now in his fifties, the man in question still draws inspiration from his childhood goal of using Tintin's adventures as a blueprint for life, and it seems to have worked for him. For some people, hitting their twenties or thirties suddenly sends them on a brief U-turn when faced with the responsibilities of adulthood, and they'll find themselves yearning for the comforts of their youth. When I returned to England at age forty-three, after living abroad for over twenty years, I began reading comics again for the first time since I was a kid, and purchasing the occasional vintage action figure. I came to realize that it was a way of reconnecting with my roots. Since I have little knowledge of my family heritage, it makes sense that I began to re-explore my original interests. I also became obsessed with the band Queen (*Flash Gordon* was the first vinyl record I owned and the soundtrack to my childhood), after only ever having a general appreciation for them. What soon followed was accomplishing my childhood dreams of becoming an actor, and writing a book. But all of this isn't merely an observation on a yearning to fulfil youthful dreams. It's an exercise in developing creativity, and tuning in to our true nature. One of wonder, one of love, and a sense of possibility. Children play. Animals of higher intelligence play. Why do we stop? Take note of how you use your free time. By tuning in to our childhood selves, we can connect with our intuition and our original life goals, or our soul plan, you remember? The stuff you wanted to do before life got in the way. And it really comes down to this: Would your eight-year-old self be proud of the life you are currently living?

Meditation Exercise: The Play's the Thing.
Level: Intermediate

Before we begin, I want to mention that not everyone's childhood is filled with playful memories. We carry trauma from our early years, and my own upbringing was fraught with my biological father's terrible abuse of my mother, and then conflict between myself and my stepdad. Childhood can be difficult to revisit. Therapy is a useful tool to work through emotions that may arise when we explore and focus on our past. The meditation that follows is in no way designed to reopen old wounds, or as a substitute for seeking professional psychiatric help.

Once again, familiarize yourself with the text before following the instructions. Better still, record yourself reading it, leaving a few beats between each verse, and play it back.

1. Find yourself a quiet place to sit and unwind, where you will remain undisturbed for at least ten minutes. Focus on your breath, and let your shoulders and belly relax. Let your jaw soften, as you continue to bring your awareness to the natural rhythm of your breath. You begin to feel safe and rested. Your back is supported, your arms are heavy and still, and with each breath you begin to settle deeper into your chair.

2. Now, bring to mind a place from your childhood where you felt secure and safe. A place such as your old bedroom, or the garden. Perhaps it was a relative's house, or that of a childhood friend. I want you to imagine this safe area in as much detail as you can, and I want you to picture yourself there, as you are now, fully grown. You're dressed comfortably, perhaps in a favorite old pair of pyjamas or loose-fitting, warm clothes. You are in a place free from worries, a safe space, a place where you can use your imagination to conjure the past, and take a relaxed, nostalgic walk down memory lane. Look around the space and try to recall as many objects as possible. Maybe imagine how soft the couch feels, or if you're outside, the smell of the dirt and grass in summer. Remember any toys scattered around or your favorite doll. Simply recall

anything and everything from this safe, happy, childhood place. Don't force it, just let the memories flow. If other thoughts creep in, simply acknowledge them, let them move along, and return to the safe space from your past.

3. You are anchored there now, and free to take a walk around. Look at everything that surrounds you as your imagination blends with the past, and brings it all to this present moment. Perhaps there's the sound of the breeze gently brushing through the trees. Perhaps the radio's on in the kitchen. Maybe you can hear your mom singing in the next room. You feel safe, you feel relaxed, and you're happy to be back here again. It's been so long.

4. After you have finished exploring, I want you to take something you found, perhaps a favorite toy, and walk out of the house, or the park, or the garden, wherever your space is, and to the street outside. Don't worry, you'll be back soon, you're just going on a little adventure. The street is exactly as you remember it, but now you're adult size. Walk down the street, remembering all the details you can of the surrounding buildings. Is there a neighbor's house that you recall? Are there any sounds? Maybe a dog is barking in the distance or there is the sound of children playing at a local school. A neighborhood cat wanders by and circles around a mailbox a couple of times before darting into a bush. And now you notice multicolored flags and fairy lights strung through the fences and trees. It looks as though there's been a street fair recently, leftover signs that everyone's been having a lovely time. As you continue along the sidewalk, you see an old movie theatre right at the end of the street. And as you get a little closer, you realize it's the one you used to go to as a kid. Your parents would take you there, or you'd go with friends. It doesn't matter that it's in a different place. It's

right there, and the doors are open and the smell of all your favorite treats entices you closer.

5. There's no one behind the concession stand, and you are free to browse and help yourself. It's all for you. So you grab some of your best-loved treats, and walk through the old cinema towards one of the theatres at the back. Perhaps there are posters on the walls of movies you saw with your childhood friends or parents. You stop to take a look at them before continuing on to the screening room.

6. You open the door, and enter the auditorium. The lights are on, and there's no one else there. But you're good, you're safe. The cool smell of the auditorium floods your entire body with a deep sense of nostalgia. You've got your favorite toy and your favorite snacks, and you find the best seat in the house, and sit down to wait for the movie to begin.

7. The lights go down, and the screen illuminates. There on the movie screen, you see yourself when you were a child. You see images of when you were a baby, being cared for by your mother or guardian. You see your parents' delight as you took your first steps, and their laughter at some of the goofy things you did and said. There's your bedroom, and you're settling down for the night while a grown-up reads you a story. Perhaps your siblings are there too. The images on the screen move forward through time. Next you're on a family vacation, everyone looks so happy! You can almost taste the air from that trip, and it evokes such warm and pleasing memories as you sit here in the empty theatre, watching the movie of your own life. It's beautiful. A private screening just for you, and some of the things you're seeing you haven't thought of in years! Grandparents and old friends are up there on the screen. There is nothing but love and laughter

and good times. So many good times when life was free and the world was wide open. The movie moves forward some more. You're older now, maybe seven or eight, and you're playing your favorite games with your childhood friends. There's nothing to worry about, there's nothing else that needs to be done. All that's happening up there on the screen is pure enjoyment, abandonment, just playtime. You see places that you had forgotten about, you see flashes of other games and other sunny days and bike rides and pets and Saturday morning cartoons. There are the summer holidays that seemed to go on for months and months, and you were loved, unconditionally and always. There were the first sparks of a childhood crush, there were weekends at the mall or exploring the local woods, and there's even the movie theatre you are sitting in right now, playing that movie you went to see as a kid. You see yourself bedding down for the night and remembering the sounds of the TV while your parents stayed up to watch the late night shows. It's comforting, it's safe. It's your heritage and your upbringing. All the characters from your early life, looking healthy, looking happy, looking vital and young.

8. Everyone that's been in the movie is onscreen now. They're all facing the camera and are waving at you, all of those you loved, all of those who loved you. Up there on the screen, they're smiling and waving at you from the past. They're pleased with you for coming back to see them, and you're up there too, the little you, right in the middle and waving back at you in the here and now. That little you is amazed at how far you've come, and so thankful to see you all grown up. But it's time for them to go now, and with big grins all round they give you one

more wave before turning to walk back to the past. The screen fades to black, and the house lights come up.

9. You get up from your cinema seat and leave the screening room, going out of the movie theatre and back down the street. The sun's beginning to set, and you're heading home. All the fairy lights that lined the fences and trees are lit up and sparkling now in the twilight. They're guiding you back to your safe place. Back to the garden, back to your auntie's place, or back to your childhood house. Heading back to your safe space and replacing the talisman you took with you to the movie theatre. Remember? The toy you've been carrying with you all this time. It'll be right here next time you come back, and you can come back as often as you wish.

10. Bring your attention back to your breath, and to the here and now. Inhale deeply, become aware of any sounds around you, feel the ground beneath you, and wiggle your fingers and toes. The past is alive inside you and time isn't what we think it is. Use this visualization exercise whenever you need to connect with your childhood self.

Chapter Four: Time after Time

Did you know, that time passes more slowly for our feet, than it does for our heads? It's true. Time moves faster for someone living in the northern hemisphere than it does for someone in the south. Time is slowed by the Earth, or that which we call gravity. A clock on the top floor of a high rise building moves faster than one on the ground floor. So which one is the actual time? Neither. And both. Because both times move relative to each other. And it goes even further than that. By scientific fact, as we currently understand it, there isn't one actual consistent time, or even two. There is a different time for every single point in continuous existence, that are each and all relative to one another. According to Einstein, there are a multitude of events all affecting other events, and that is how he explained time in his Theory of Relativity that I've briefly touched on above. His equations don't delineate one single consistent moment of time, but multifarious times. To whittle this idea down to its most basic soundbites, everything moves with its own rhythm, and everyone marches to the beat of their own drum.

So, that's the easy part out of the way. The next part is our relationship with linear time. And that's where things, for me at least, get tricky. We can count the number of times the Earth goes around the Sun, just as we've done for thousands of years. This shows us the linear progress from a starting point onward. Or we can measure the vibration of caesium-133 atoms, which sets something called International Atomic Time, the global standard that is apparently so precise, it will take 1.4 million years for it to be off by a second. In the latter half of my thirties, I experienced what I believe was an awakening to ultimate reality, or time outside of time as we know it. Now this may sound a little grandiose, or that I'm implying I've experienced something that others haven't. This isn't the case. We all have the ability to experience this phenomena. In fact it happens spontaneously, when time appears to slow down in an emergency, or when you catch yourself on the spot and breathe and realize that just for a second, there is nothing but now. And we can expand on this. It simply requires a shift in the way we look at our relationship with the models of time we've highlighted so far.

I awoke one morning with the realization that time wasn't what I'd thought it was, and the linear process that we all adhere to suddenly made no sense to me. We only ever experience the present moment. Everything else is either a memory of the past or an idea about the future, and we get lost in it. We drift through our days in our heads without ever connecting to the here and now. And it's now all the time, right? We can only ever experience real time, right now, and then that moment of real time has vanished and been measured and logged in our memories and we are on to the next. Well this thought sent me into a spiral. A literal spiral. Because I quickly realized that as well as being linear, time itself is a paradox that is also an ever-turning spiral of now. Going nowhere and everywhere simultaneously. Looked at this way, it meant that everything that has ever happened is happening right now, and everything that could happen is infinite. Unbeknownst to me at the time, I was experiencing what the 7th century Buddhist Tantras referred to as "primordial time". The ultimate state of deathless awareness. A state of reality in which we become nobody and remain as we are simultaneously. The time before we become somebody, the eternal time of primordial purity. Not past, present, or future, but eternal time. In this everlasting time, we were, as well as we are, and we will be luminous awareness. We glow.

I went mad for awhile. I couldn't switch it off. I felt trapped in this timeless moment of awareness, the constant moment of now not moving with linear time, and I was terrified. Doctors

were of no use, they simply dismissed my ramblings as a
mental breakdown, or temporary psychosis. This diagnosis,
by the way, is common in spiritual breakthroughs. One of my
teachers, James Van Praagh, author of numerous books and a
world-renowned medium, talks of this routinely on his YouTube
channel. The book *Breaking Down Is Waking Up*, by psychiatrist
Dr. Russell Razzaque, also covers this subject in depth. In recent
years, many other teachings are coming to light about living in
the "5th Dimension", which is essentially what I was having
first-hand experience of. Over the course of a year or two, I
eventually grew used to this new perspective and learned first
how to live with it, and then sway it towards my advantage.
I began to realize that I could focus on things with laser-like
precision when needed. When I tap into it, I feel as though I am
in a limitless state of being, unconstrained by how we've set
time up. Out of time. For the most part I play by the rules we've
made to function in society. I still drift off into my thoughts and
get caught up in life's dramas and emotions. I still experience
things the same way that we all do. But I seem to have the
ability to step out of it. And in those moments of what I believe
to be ultimate awareness of ultimate reality, time, ageing, and
even death seem to be nothing more than constructs to get us
through this current physical phase of our soul's evolution.

I believe I can point you towards achieving this state also.
There's nothing to be afraid of. Your experience won't be the
rude awakening that I had. You won't go crazy. We are taking
baby steps here, and we shall ease into a way of thinking that
will simply be an alternative idea to the generally agreed upon,
popular one.

In contrast to being able to tune in to the present moment,
in recent years I've felt acutely aware of the past. More than
aware, it's as though I can go there. Now before I start sounding
completely bonkers, I want to stress that I don't believe I can

time travel! But what I'm talking about is being able to somehow tap in to the past and feel it, smell it, taste it. It's truly like being there again. This ability seems to have developed with little effort on my part, and I wonder if it's the opposite correlation to the experience of tuning in to the now. I don't know. I've talked to others about it, and much like when I was attempting to explain my experience of living in the now, I'm met with blank faces. I'm not talking about remembering a special occasion vividly, like we all do, and I'm not claiming to be able to recall everything I've ever witnessed. When it happens, it can be overwhelming, and trigger personal emotions. It's really like being right *there*. Having thought it over, it seems likely that if I am supposedly destined to become a voice for Spirit, as I'm repeatedly told by those further along the journey than me, then being able to vividly connect with both the past and present would be a useful skill.

Let's get to it.

Being able to step back from our thoughts and observe them, like we have talked about earlier, can be used to our advantage when developing skills to tune in to the present moment and connect with the past. The exercises we have done so far have taught us to do exactly that. In fact I've only just realized this, which makes me believe that my Guides are stepping in again, just like in Book One. The exercise "All The Feels" in Chapter Two taught us how to connect with our present self and step back to observe the thoughts we were projecting on to the screen. The next exercise, "The Play's The Thing", taught us to be both present in the past and then separate from and witness the past while sitting in the auditorium *of* our past.

Before we go any further, let's talk about the three levels of awareness in the mind. The subconscious, the conscious, and the superconscious. You've heard these terms before, but let's quickly reacquaint ourselves with ourselves. The subconscious is operating without our awareness, taking care of bodily functions such as breathing and swallowing, assessing our environments and movements etc. The conscious is what we focus on, responding to our environment, concentrating on our concerns, and it is able to override some subconscious jobs, such as controlling our breath. The superconscious transcends ordinary consciousness. It is our intuition, the consciousness that connects to ultimate reality, the universe, and Spirit. It is able to override some subconscious jobs, when we get to the point of becoming aware that we are aware, or when a medium channels Spirit.

Alright, so now we know the three levels of awareness, let's go back to the example of the first exercise. Our thoughts, memories of the past, dreams of the future, and our autonomous subconscious, are all constantly projecting images on the screen. Those that we choose to focus on, such as our plans for the day ahead, and those that are in our immediate environment that we occasionally turn our attention to, such as our physical presence and external influences (walking, eating, watching TV etc.). We use the conscious part of our mind to focus the projector and concentrate on the movie on the screen, while our superconscious mind, the part that is forever external to the constraints of time, quietly watches from behind the scenes. If we are able to access the superconscious, the quiet observer, then we can pay attention to the conscious and subconscious and bring the superconscious out from behind the scenes, aligning all three with the present moment. When all three are aligned, we are as ultimately aware as we can be in this physical state. We are truly living in the now, because body, mind and soul are in unison.

Respectively, the same construct applies to connecting with the past. We'll use the example of the second exercise, when we visualized our safe space and then went for a walk to the movies. First of all, we took our conscious thoughts into the past with a visualization exercise. We imagined ourselves there, as we are now, and we could smell the air and taste the sweets that we ate. For all intents and purposes, our consciousness was there while our subconscious continued to sit and breathe in physical reality. Then we watched the events of our childhood play out on the cinema screen. Our superconscious took the reins, we connected ourselves to it by sitting it in the auditorium with a toy and popcorn, and we let it watch the images up on the screen that the conscious mind played out. If you had a physical reaction to the exercise, if it brought up emotions while you sat in the present while simultaneously living in the past, then you briefly demonstrated bringing all levels of awareness into unison. Where we shall go with our next exercise is to practice bringing all three levels of consciousness into complete awareness of the here and now.

In Book Three of this series we shall bring another player into the game, Ultimate Awareness itself, also described by some as the "supraconscious": When we connect the superconscious to the Divine, and we are aware that we are aware that we are aware of our thoughts. When the "I am me" analogy comes into play that was mentioned in the previous book, and we look at the I from the All That Is, and the I becomes the All. When we step back from our thoughts and watch them, without reacting, and then step back even further. When you shall stand side by side with your Guides, and your Guides with their Guides.

OK, then. I believe that my Spirit Guides just joined us. This is news to me! I look forward to that. I have no idea how I shall write from experience since I don't believe I have experienced what we were just told. I need to read it again. I also just learned that Spirit Guides have Spirit Guides. I need to ask one of my teachers about that. I guess we really are "glowing deeper". I need to take a break...

Meditation Exercise: Present Presence. Level: All levels

For our first exercise in connecting with the present, we'll start by simply blending with our immediate environment through the sounds around us. As we progress through this book, we will take things a little further to connect with the everlasting moment of now.

Note: if you have a hearing impairment simply follow instructions 1, 2, and 6. Alternate between bringing your attention to your breath, and the feeling of your heartbeat.

1. Sit in a comfortable position with a straight back. Close your eyes, and take three deep, grounding breaths, either through your nose or mouth, whichever you prefer. Now let your breathing return to normal and simply pay attention to it for a few moments. If your brain attempts to distract you with random thoughts, just bring your focus back to your breathing.

2. Begin to notice your heartbeat. Feel it in your chest, and notice the beautiful symmetry between your heart beating and your breath flowing in and out. Out of synch but completely in unison. Meditate on your heartbeat. Your mother's heartbeat was the first thing you experienced in your suspended state in the womb. Even if you are unable to physically hear, you can still tune in to your own rhythm of your heart and your breath. The breath flows in and then out. The heart dictates the rhythm of your life, and can always connect you back to your original home, the heartbeat that your mother passed from herself to you. Take time to sit with them now, and explore the deeper connections that you have with both.

3. Now begin to notice the sounds in your environment. In fact, take all of your attention to the sounds in your environment. Imagine that for the time being, it is your only sense. Scan the world around you for sound. Notice as many as you can. Spend a few seconds on each sound and then move to the next. Don't give them a back story. Simply hear them, note them, and move on. A clock ticking. A car passing by. A dog barking. A door being slammed. The washing machine whirring.

4. Slowly, expand your hearing to distant sounds. Maybe there's a train rolling by somewhere far away. Perhaps there's the laughter of children in a playground across town. Focus for a few seconds on each sound, zoom in on it with your ears. Let the other sounds fall away as your focus becomes laser-like and moves across great distances to experience that sound in the here and now. All you are doing is listening, and being aware.

5. Now bring your awareness back to your breath, and pay attention to it. Listen to the sound of your breathing and let it connect you with your place in the world, here and now. Let all of the sounds around you blend with the sound of your breath. Whatever sounds arise, simply take note of them in an unbroken stream of awareness of the ongoing moment of now. There is only now.

6. When you are ready, let the sounds drift back out to your peripheral awareness and bring your attention back to your physical self, sitting in the present moment. Feel your feet on the floor, feel your hands on your lap or the arms of the chair. Become aware of any itches or glitches throughout your body. Take a deep breath, and open your eyes.

Chapter Five: 5D

People are experiencing a shift in perspective. Such an occurrence may have brought you to this book, or your intuition is guiding you in search of one. This is happening at a personal level to millions across the globe, but it's also happening collectively. Think about it. The world is a different place to what it was a few years ago. Not just in terms of wars, global warming, and experiencing a pandemic, but in all areas. As a species, we are evolving into more advanced versions of our former selves. There is talk in spiritual communities regarding the "upgrade" we are all going through as our conscious awareness shifts from material 3D to metaphysical 5D. The Greek philosopher Plato wrote of what he believed to be an alternate realm beyond our 3D material world. He called this the World of Forms, a plane of absolute truth which was later interpreted as the Euclidean 4th Dimension, and includes Einstein's concept of SpaceTime. We are now beginning to move beyond 4D, and are awakening into a higher state of consciousness. For those of us who are energetically in tune with this shift, it will involve being able to access more of our extrasensory perceptions. Things like clairaudience (hearing sounds or voices from other dimensions), psychic and mediumistic abilities, tuning into the present moment with laser-like precision, or being able to see auras and feel shifts in energy. These are just some of the abilities we will be able to tune in to if we take the time to raise our vibration. Ultimately, now is a time of spiritual evolution.

I hate labels. I hate the term "5D", but it's been the current buzz-term for awhile now so let's go with it. Mark my words, someone's going to write a book soon, or make a documentary and stick it on Gaia, and call it "Living In 6D" or "10D". Maybe they'll go straight to "20D" to get ahead of the curve, who knows. But for now everyone's concerned about moving to the 5th. So let's break the states of 3D, 4D, and 5D down to a personal level. By doing this we can see where we are on the spectrum of spiritual growth as we currently understand it.

Living in the 3rd Dimension is essentially what the majority of the human race have been doing since gaining self-awareness. Someone living in this state believes that they are relying solely on their five senses to navigate each day and nothing more. They identify themselves purely as the product of genetics and the circumstances they have so far experienced, and connect their identity to their social status, material wealth, and belongings. Life may be viewed as a competition, and the survival of the fittest. There is a great comfort to living in the 3rd Dimension, since what you see is what you get. There is no need to dig deeper or search for higher truths. The general consensus of group solidarity and belief is enough. But some traumas may be more difficult to manage in this state. Failing to look beyond surface level living can result in not exploring meanings behind certain behaviors or reactions. Anger, jealousy, fear and grief may never be healed. It is possible to move beyond the 3rd Dimension and into the 4th or 5th, since at a soul level, we already have the blueprint, the "soul plan", and ability to awaken further.

The interpretation of the 4th Dimension at a personal level means that someone is more open to higher states of consciousness than in the 3D state. At a physical level, one may begin to care more for their health and well-being than they did prior to awakening in 4D. The same goes for the environment and their fellow planet dwellers. They will be able to slip between 3D and 4D with ease, choosing to engage in higher truths for a time, or completely ignoring them in favor of the convenience of a more comfortable existence. 4D, however, is the gateway to the next state, and someone living at this level of awareness will experience calls to action and a desire to look beyond the veil of physical reality. There will be a strong yearning to explore purpose and passions, rather than accepting a conventional way of living. Work will have to be fulfilling. Intuition has the potential to expand and a connection to a Higher Plane will seem plausible beyond current scientific fact. Science and spirituality will no longer seem mutually exclusive. A deeper meaning will be sought, and insights into human behavior and reactions will be understood with continuing evolution. They will be aware that they have awoken, but they may not demonstrate with their day-to-day actions that they *are* awoken. It is possible to move beyond the 4th Dimension and into the 5th, since at a soul level, we already have the blueprint, the "soul plan", and ability to awaken further.

Living in 5D means not being able to go back. If you awaken to a 5D state too quickly, you may experience panic, and an initial reluctance of this new perception. But with time you will adjust, and conceive all three states and be able to function day to day. Being able to perceive the world from the predominantly 3D state, while living from a 5D state, and being able to navigate it as such will greatly serve you and those around you. Friends and family may initially become impatient with you when you begin to talk of your new perception. They may not be able to grasp your personal truths, and could dismiss your views as "New-Age mumbo-jumbo" or as being detached from reality. You will find greater meaning and reward from all life circumstances, including recognizing the lessons in negative ones. You will no longer identify yourself as your occupation or culmination of experiences. Working a conventional nine-to-five job may no longer be satisfactory. You will recognize each individual as being on their own personal journey and not judge others over their beliefs or interpretations of the world. You will see synchronicity in life circumstances. You will learn not to drift too far from intuitive truths and get lost in conspiratorial theories, feelings of superiority, or a guru complex. Buying in to every conspiracy theory and pseudoscientific debate purely because they are against the norm is not living from a place of intuitive truth. This happens when people mistakenly believe they have entered the 5th Dimension but haven't, perhaps through their own research or using psychedelics, and they experience what they believe is the 5th Dimension from their ego. When you truly awaken to it, your ego will be the first casualty. You will feel a need to inform others of this state but without enforcing your beliefs or coming from a place of condescendence. You will heed the call to become the difference that makes a difference. You will develop compassion and respect for all living beings including the Earth. Time will no longer be viewed as linear, but the linear perception will be experienced as a tool to navigate the three labelled realms of perception. You will connect with your highest self, Spirit Guides, and the All That Is on a regular basis and with growing ease. You will see this current incarnation of your physical life as part of a grander tapestry of an ever-evolving soul. Death will no longer exist. It is possible to move beyond the 5th Dimension, in fact it is a given, since at a soul level, we already have the blueprint, the "soul plan", and ability to awaken further.

So what comes next? What's beyond 5D (great book title for any aspiring 6 Dimensioners out there)? I haven't experienced what comes next. Or, to put it another way, in this current incarnation of my soul's journey, I don't remember what comes next. But I believe that we received a hint about it from my Guides at the end of the last chapter, and I am intrigued to see if that's what we shall learn about in Book Three of this series.

Chapter Six: Memory and the Mystical Experience

Almost all experiences that we have fit neatly into our memories as something we can relate to. When we experience an event in our physical, day-to-day lives, we typically have a comparison to an earlier, similar experience from the past, so we can categorize the two and file them in our memories as relatable. This generates our reaction to the most recent one, based on our previous likes or dislikes. All of this happens in an instant, and we respond accordingly. Let me give you an example. Let's say you're in the city and walking down the street. You're in a new area and following a map on your phone. You've never been there before and you are experiencing this place for the very first time. You have experienced other streets for the very first time, and although there is a slight element of the unknown and perhaps even a dull excitement to this one, you already know the drill since you have discovered hundreds of new areas throughout your lifetime. But then a loud bang interrupts your exploration. It catches you off guard and you spin around to locate the source of the noise. Your subconscious pulls out of its natural ongoing state and switches to fully conscious in order to protect you from any external threat. But you quickly realize the noise was just a large truck passing by and hitting a bump in the road. Your brain immediately detangles all of the possible harmful scenarios that it has instantly thrown at you, since it knows that large heavy trucks sometimes make such noises when they hit a speed bump, based on you having experienced this before. Truck + bump = bang. No threat. Your conscious thought turns back to the map, your subconscious relaxes and retakes its place in the backseat, and your brain puts the experience down to entropy. The noise was simply a random moment of chaos external to your personal controlled experience. It was merely a preconceived irregularity that was unexpected but nevertheless familiar in terms of everyday encounters beyond our control. We do all of the above with all things. We do it when choosing what to eat. We do it when choosing what to watch on TV. We do it when we meet someone at a party who reminds us of someone else we met at another party. We base almost everything on past experiences resulting in what we liked or didn't like at the time.

When we have a mystical experience, the brain tries to do the same thing. It recognizes the experience as new, and instantly sources its databanks to map this new experience as familiar territory. Except it's not familiar territory. These experiences sometimes come in as feelings, either a physical feeling that defies logic since there is no apparent source to create the feeling (e.g. hair on the arms standing up without a local draft, a warm tingling sensation when meditating, or the sense that someone is besides you in an empty room), or an innate sense of knowing that is purely subjective and brand new, with no previous experience to compare it with. Sometimes we see things that defy logic, such as a man standing besides your mother on your video call when she is at home alone (see Book One). The brain analyses the evidence and doesn't come up with an explanation, so it dispels the experience as nonsensical and therefore impossible. The first few times we have these moments, they tend to be dismissed. Particularly when they happen out of context to the rest of our day. If we were not expecting it, and something randomly happens that appears esoteric and makes no sense, we tend to simply take a brief note, then move on with the practical, relatable and tangible day.

My fiancée and I once shared a mystical experience when we were out one night in London. She is a self-proclaimed agnostic, leaning towards atheist. Our relationship has an interesting dynamic, particularly as I have jumped headlong into exploring the mystical and I one hundred percent believe in a Creator and life after death. Anyway, I felt what I recognized as a presence letting itself be known to us, in an old pub in Soho. It was visceral, but intangible in the common sense. I couldn't see it, but it was unmistakably there. She felt it too. I *knew* that she felt it too and I knew that she knew that I knew that she knew. Don't ask me how. But we immediately locked eyes as we felt this warm, loving presence enter our space in a semi-busy pub called The Blue Posts.

"What's going on?" Laura asked me, eyes wide.

"This is what I've been telling you about," I replied excitedly. "But it won't last long, and when it's gone we'll find it difficult to remember."

I'd experienced instances like this before but rarely with anyone else, and not for a very long time.

This friendly, glowing presence left me after a minute or so, but it stayed with Laura a little longer, and I asked her to describe what she was feeling so we could try and recall it later on.

"I don't know how to," she exclaimed with awe. "But something's happening."

Inevitably it left, and gradually the noises from the pub crept back in and we were once again in regular, everyday reality.

We had meditated together earlier that day for the very first time. I don't think it was a coincidence that this happened later that night, and I believe it was one of our Guides giving us a welcoming gift.

I assumed then, that Laura's agnostic leaning towards atheism days were done.

But it wasn't to be the case. As time went on, and the memory grew dimmer, Laura has since acknowledged that something definitely happened that night in Soho which she couldn't explain, but it makes no difference whatsoever to her personal belief in any kind of afterlife.

As your intuition grows, and you actively seek out the esoteric and connect with your own Spirit Guides, the experiences you may have once fleetingly had will occur with more frequency.

Over time, you will have too many of them to put down to wishful thinking or imagination. They still won't sit in your memory the same way that everyday occurrences will. But you will be able to start comparing them when they happen more often. Not only that, when you start to accept these experiences as real, for example journeying in a meditative state, you will gain insights from them through your conscious reasoning, rather than not knowing what to do with them. While there may never be empirical data to prove these occurrences to the masses, it doesn't mean that they aren't subjectively real. And what is subjectively real to thousands and thousands of people should surely be evidence enough. After all, isn't what is seen and experienced as objective reality on the outside merely a reflection of the subjective reality within? Whether individually or collectively? Alas, that's not the way we have the world set up. I've had too many of these occurrences to attribute to hallucination or grief or whatever other logical explanation a skeptic might throw at me, or indeed my own doubts. Have your own mystical experiences and lead the way.

Here's a quick example to combine all of the above. Have you ever seen one of those drawings where the image changes dependent on the viewer? You know the ones, when one moment the drawing appears to be a rabbit looking to the left, and then the next you see a duck looking to the right. What were rabbit ears become the duck's beak. Everything about it looks different, yet nothing has changed. If you grew up in the 90s, there were those 3D hologram pictures that at first looked like a bunch of colorful dots, but revealed a hidden image if you readjusted your eyes. Well it's kind of like that. Not everyone can see it. Or some people see a duck and some see a rabbit. Everyone's experience comes from their own perspective, or through their own lens. We are each on our individual paths and we must be respectful of others. We are not here to preach, and as frustrating as it may be we can't expect everyone to agree with our model of the world. Carry the flame and be the light for all. Perspective shapes potential. They may not see the flame, and it might even take you some time to see it too, but there is still wisdom burning within it.

Chapter Seven: Pardon the Intrusion

I know that I'm like a broken record with this "you are not your thoughts" thing. But I can't stress it enough. It has the potential to make a wild difference to your everyday reality and spiritual growth when you can implement this concept into your daily life without having to try. Even if you're on the fence about mediumship, these initial chapters on learning to identify our thoughts as separate from our Higher Selves will serve you to no end. So before we move away from self-development for awhile (In the next part of this book we're going to look at esoteric teachings from a wider angle. We shall still be able to apply them to our own growth, but we shall have a short break before we delve into connecting with our Spirit Guides and further developing our intuition.), I want to talk once again about the practice of not confusing yourself, your authentic self, with your thoughts.

Despite what we may think, we don't really create our thoughts. We can mold them, we can direct them, but for the most part we become aware of them when they enter autonomously from our subconscious, or are inspired by our environment. For our entire lives, we have been arguing with them, repressing them, trying to ignore them, pushing them to the background, mistrusting them, and believing them. What we've been learning to do in these pages, is how to step back from them, how to observe them, and how to choose which ones we let go of or use for our benefit. Creation comes from inspiration, inspiration propagates intention, and thought produces the means to the outcome.

We don't always get to choose what thoughts pop into our heads, but we can choose to acknowledge or disregard them. We can enjoy a thought and run with it. We can imagine possible outcomes and fantasize with them. We can use them to connect with memories of the past and spend time with them. They truly are a beautiful thing. But they can also become irrational, feed fears, and become obsessive.

The psychological fields of mental health and medicine use the term "intrusive" to describe negative thoughts and doubts that can prove counterproductive to our well-being and accomplishing positive outcomes in our day-to-day lives. But the truth is that *all* thoughts are intrusive. They're coming in night and day whether we are conscious of them or not. They're there when we wake up, they're there when we go to work, they're there when we have conversations, they're there when we eat, they're there when we watch TV, they're there when we sleep. We can't stop them. We can't get away from them. They're constantly intruding, whether we perceive them as positive or negative. So we may as well get used to them. It's how we choose to respond to them that is key. Our relationship with our thoughts is what needs to change, since we can't regulate the thoughts themselves. But we can regulate our reactions to them. A negative thought can be just as productive as a positive one. A negative or obsessive thought can be the catalyst to change. Negative thoughts can become the building blocks of a positive outcome. A negative thought is simply a reminder of an area in our lives that needs work, and it's presenting itself from the darkest recesses of our consciousness to let us know that we can create a change if we choose to. Instead of trying to repress the negative thought, step back and observe it. Don't attach any emotion to it. Just see what it's trying to let you know. Is it irrational? Then fine, recognize it as that and let it slide right on by. It'll soon get tired of showing up, even if it's obsessive (and most obsessive thoughts are irrational); it'll give up when you don't give it power. Simply observe it. Does it make sense? Does it serve your higher good? If it does neither then let it go, the same as you would a stranger on the street shouting at you for no good reason. It's a screwball, it doesn't know the real you, the you who simply observes it and walks away. Leave it screaming for your attention and move on. Feel free to engage it and assess it, but attach no emotion to it, and address it or leave it. Negative thoughts promoting anxiety and fear are from deep, deep places we haven't dealt with yet. They're asking for help, essentially. They're lessons from the past that we never dealt with. They're negative influential people who made us doubt ourselves when we were vulnerable. They're not you. But they can be used to create a better you. They are the crude material that you can craft into the best version of yourself that is out there waiting for you to choose you. The best you. Don't suppress or bury them. Look at them, and see if they are worth crafting, and if they are not, let them pass right on by.

You are not your thoughts.

When we have an idea, thought, or inspiration, it takes shape as a possibility in our mind. It also takes shape in the greater consciousness of the Universal Mind. The All That Is. God. The Great Mystery. Pangu. Thanos, Whoever you choose to attribute to Universal Consciousness. The thought we have has the potential to expand beyond our own consciousness and to that of Universal Consciousness. So we want to make sure that what we pay attention to is what we want to send out to the wider world. And we can't do that by suppressing or obsessing over negative thoughts. They will arise. So we acknowledge them and move on. Or address them and take the necessary actions to heal them. And let me clearly reiterate the fact that we cannot banish all negative thinking and view life as perfect no matter what happens. We have no choice but to think. Thought breeds creation. We manifest that which we think into reality. We are able to see a chair in our mind's eye and then build it. We see the route to work in our memory and then we take it. We see ourselves getting the new job and we get it. Some teachers of manifestation methods choose to discourage negative thinking entirely, but it's a losing battle, we cannot stop negative thoughts. We need to learn to recognize our thoughts and dance between them. Observations are not negation. Thinking or stating facts won't instantly inhibit your potential to live your best life. Declaring statistics about the horrors in the world won't make those horrors worse. Talking about school shootings or having a conversation about Global Warming won't manifest more school shootings or expand the holes in the Ozone Layer over the Tropics and Antarctic. It's our thoughts about ourselves that we need to be conscious of, because they have the ability to block our desired outcomes. What we concentrate on in our own lives, we create in our own lives. Our thoughts have the potential to blend with the All That Is, and that action has the potential to help us flow towards that which we desire. Remember: we can exist on autopilot and cultivate a life of banality, or we can live with intent and choose the direction. We are not our thoughts. We are the ones observing our thoughts, and every wonderful possibility that you can imagine is out there waiting for you to choose it.

Our thoughts are based on our perceptions, and our perceptions are based on past experiences and are the default setting of our belief systems. Until you purposefully activate your intuition, almost everything that you perceive, both consciously and subconsciously, is filtered through what you've decided as your truth to this point. And what you've decided on as your truth to this point, and what influences your perception of the world, is what you've experienced so far and what you've turned your attention to. Think about it. That which has created who you believe yourself to be, is simply a result of what you once focused on, and circumstance. That's it. That's how most of us cruise through this life. We chose to look left instead of right. We chose to go here instead of there. If we had gone there instead of here, our perception would be different. The experience would have been different, and our thoughts and views of the world would be different to what they are today. We are born into perception. No matter if we are born with or without sight, the gift of hearing, two legs, two arms, and ten fingers and toes, we physically perceive the world through the senses we are blessed with. We deal with what we've got from day one.

But there may come a time in life when we recognize we have another option when it comes to perceiving our environment. There is a subtler world beneath the physical appearance of the one we have all agreed upon, and there is a way to tune in to it: To actively boot up our intuition. We have already been using it without knowing it for our entire lives. And when we consciously awaken it, we have a chance to start over again, and see the world with eyes anew. Once you've done this, you can't go back. The veil has been lifted. And it's important to know that this is how things truly are, in ultimate reality. There is a sparkling rainbow slipstream superhighway running alongside the mundane world right now, waiting for you to see it and embrace it, hoping that you will jump on and enjoy the ride. It's happening whether you choose to acknowledge it or not. It is a deeper reality. And when you have seen it, you cannot unsee it. You simply need to learn how to step back from your thoughts, and find the spaces in between. To recognize those spaces, you need to get used to sitting in the silence, and stepping back from thoughts. Observe them, and only react if there is the potential to create a positive outcome. Otherwise let the thought go, and look beyond it. It is there where intuition begins.

Part Two: Nature, the Mystical Occult, and the Multiverse

Chapter Eight: Bridging the Gap between Nature Spirits, Ceremony, and Earth Energy

Let's take our foot off the pedal for a short while. Let's do something different to what we did in the first book. We dove headfirst into spiritual metaphysics and we're building on the topics from *Letting Glow*. But let's not run before we can walk. Let's take a breath.

I've already thrown a lot at you, particularly in the last chapter, so let's have a little fun while we learn about other practices of tuning our intuition in to Spirit and connecting with sacred energies. Let's delve into some ancient beliefs and customs, let's talk about witches, Pagans, and poltergeists. Damn. I missed a great book title right there! Or a really bad band name.

All of what we shall learn in this section can be applied to our spiritual growth. And I believe that some of the things we'll talk about here will be crucial in understanding larger truths that will come in Book Three. But we're going to change the angle for awhile around personal development, and look at some alternate viewpoints, particularly from the past.

I believe that during these current times, there is a definite global shift in perspective, and that the practical, consumer obsessed West are opening up to the possibilities of expanding our consciousness and blending it with the energies of the Earth and those in the Spirit World. But many people still do not buy into this idea. While I eagerly awaited the publication of *Letting Glow*, I would at first be congratulated by friends on the achievement, and then the conversation would naturally turn to what the book was about. It was there that I was met with varying responses. And that's fine, I expect that. We are each responsible for the content we create and send out to the world. Anyone who makes themselves a public figure is open to the opinions of others, it's part of the territory. The subjects that we are exploring in these books are all too easy to poke fun at from someone who might be more practically driven, and in this next chapter, talking about Faeries, poltergeists and Pagan beliefs are an easy target for anyone who might dismiss them as children's tales. But to casually disregard the folklores surrounding the energies of the Earth would be a huge error, for these tales of wishing wells, witches and ancient beliefs are deeply ingrained in medicine, culture, and the very elements of our own sustenance. As well as being a guiding map to take the Earth out of its current crisis, it's also interesting to note how these culturally significant folktales compare with others from around the world. In our collective heritage, there are too many similarities to ignore.

There is wisdom in the past, and in the metaphysics that we shall soon talk about. We can apply this wisdom to our growth as modern mystics. So while we shall have some fun, I approach these topics with reverence and intrigue. I have much to learn, and the very point of these books is for us to learn together. As we float towards Higher Consciousness and connection with the astral planes, we must also embrace the fact that we are physical beings. And while I strive to make clear distinctions between the physical and spiritual, I must pay equal attention to our relationship with our environment. The spiritual and the physical are forever entwined and waltzing to the beautiful dance of life. There is not one without the other, and the two are always entangled as we evolve and move from this world to the next and back again. We are here, we are now, and we are alive in physical form. We connect with others physically as well as intellectually and spiritually, and we connect with the Earth in the same way. The disconnect comes when we lean more towards one than the other, and that is what I believe to be part of the root cause of all suffering in the world; when we are so wrapped up in the physical, that we neglect the spiritual, and when we consume and grow gluttonous at the expense of others and the planet itself. Likewise, through our religions and pursuit of spiritual evolution, we must be cautious that we don't become detached from our common physical experience.

We are sentient beings, and we share compassion for all living things. But we have moved away from this. We have been told by our scientists that our natural state is to fight for survival. That we are a selfish breed whose primary objective is to multiply and thrive at all costs, and that is why the world is in the current state that it's in. No one can deny the latter part of that statement. But recent studies have shown that we may have gotten the fundamentals all wrong. Darwin's quote "survival of the fittest" has been used by science over and over again to demonstrate nature's ruthlessness in its pursuit to procreate and evolve. But he only mentions this term once in his *Descent of Man*. We now know that our bodies recognize stress and anger as unnatural states, resulting in harmful physical reactions. The enzymes that break down fats and detoxify prescription drugs are also negatively impacted by stress. Whereas our reactions to kindness, democracy, and love, flood our systems with the primary feel-good chemicals dopamine, serotonin, oxytocin and endorphins. It is seeming more likely that our ability to sympathize with our fellow planet dwellers is an evolutionary trait that has allowed us to live and evolve to this very point in time. Not winning the argument. Not hoarding money or material things. Not going to war. Survival of the fittest, arguably deemed as scientific fact, is beginning to emerge as a myth.

Nature doesn't take more than it needs. A wolf doesn't kill more than it requires to survive, and if it does, the bounty is utilized by other animals. Birds fly in unison, and everything naturally moves in a democratic cycle. The whole supports the individual, and the individual the whole. When there is an imbalance, the cycle is jolted. Our ancient predecessors knew this, and lived in harmony with the land for the greater good of the planet and future generations.

The Pagan

When we talk of European Celts or Pagans, we are usually referring to the tribes and beliefs that were found throughout Europe and the Mediterranean prior to Roman and Christian rule. Tribes or cultures like the Gauls, Celts, Goths, and Vikings were considered Pagan. They typically had anthropomorphic gods and spirits who ruled over nature or were derived from nature, meaning they humanized their deities. Shamanism refers to the ancient tribalistic and spiritual healing practices of North, Central, and Southern America (as well as the ancient beliefs of European tribes in Siberia, Finland, and other regions with nomadic or tribal ancestries). Shamanistic belief systems do not typically anthropomorphize their gods, although it isn't a rule. The Shaman sees Spirit in nature's landscapes, plants, and animals. The spirit of an animal possessing a human is within Shamanic beliefs. Both Pagans and Shamans believe in Nature Spirits, but in the British Isles we like to put faces to the names.

The traditional Elementals of Pagan mythology can be classified in accordance with each of the four elements of Earth. Gnomes (earth), Undines (water), Salamanders (fire) and Sylphs (air). But there are many other types of Fae and offspring of the Elementals who show up in children's tales and Pagan lore around our own homes and in nature. Take the Undines of Roman mythology for example, they were water Nymphs who inhabited sacred springs. And in the Arthurian legend of

England, The Lady of the Lake is the spirit who receives the sword Excalibur. Fishermen and pirates told tales of ocean Nymphs known as Mermaids. And the Scots called water spirits the Kelpies.

Dryads are tree spirits. They can leave their tree for short periods of time at night when the tree is resting. They are known to have strong energies that can give us the feelings of uneasiness we may experience when walking through a forest alone, and it is said that if you have a favorite tree, you are most likely unknowingly enchanted with that tree's Dryad.

Pixies are a race of nature spirit who enjoy the UK coasts of Cornwall and Devon. They inhabit caves, valleys, and moors, and spend their time stealing ponies and confusing lone country walkers. They dress in green with pointy hats, or run about in their birthday suits.

Hobs and Brownies are household Sprites who were known in the British Isles to help out on the farm at night in olden days, churning butter or carrying sacks of seeds. In return for their overnight help, families would leave offerings for these Gnomes such as a cup of milk on a "Brownie Stone". Leaving no offering at all was considered rude, and if you happened to catch a naked Brownie and tried to provide it with clothes, it would get offended, turn invisible, and cause havoc around the house, hurling objects at you, becoming known as a Poltergeist.

An ancient Celtic cure for some ailments would be to bathe in a well inhabited by Undines at dusk. After leaving an offering, the sufferer would walk around the well three times while holding a chicken. The patient would then sleep beside the chicken on hallowed ground for the night, and if the chicken happened to die during sleep, the person would be cured.

As cute as these stories are, they are entwined with ancient medicinal remedies and rituals. There is an old saying that when you can put your foot on seven daisies, then Spring has come.

To wear a chain of them protects the wearer from Faerie spells. Daisies are common across the world and can be found on every continent except for Antarctica. They have been linked to Venus, Aphrodite and Freya, among others. It is said that sleeping with a daisy under your pillow will encourage an absent lover to return. In ancient England, they were known as Bruisewort, and were used (as the name suggests) to treat bruises and reduce swelling. If this old medicine were used while reciting a mantra or spell, the Nature Spirits would be sure to speed along the healing process.

The dandelion is another common plant found across the globe. They are native to Eurasia, but were introduced to North America, South America, India (where it hadn't reached naturally), Australia, New Zealand and pretty much everywhere else that Europeans migrated. It's thought that the introduction of this species to North America was intentional, as people wanted a flower that reminded them of their old countries. As well as being used to make honey, coffee, to stimulate digestion and help inflammations in the body, Pagan legend says that blowing fluffy dandelion clocks releases trapped faeries who will grant a wish. But only if none are left behind. It was also said that if you picked a dandelion on St. John's Eve, it could be used to ward off witches.

Another Celtic affirmation spell was the Blackberry Spell, which you can easily practice today. Find a wild blackberry bush and pick three leaves from it. Then take a coin, the higher the denomination the better, and bind it in the leaves with thread. Wrap the parcel in cloth or place it in a pouch and keep it safe in your pocket or purse, and expect prosperity to come your way.

In Ireland, Faeries and mushrooms have always been part of Irish culture and deeply intertwined. In fact, Gaelic slang for Faeries and mushrooms is the same word: Pookies, or Pooka. The accompanying hallucinogenic trip that arises from ingesting magic mushrooms is described as being "away with the Faeries" or being "off with the Pixies".

The ancient Amerindian tribes who we typically associate with Shamanism also believed in Faeries, but saw the Elementals as magical mortals with connections to the ethereal realms. They divided their mortal supernatural companions into two categories, those connected with the glowing lights in the sky, the Star People, and those who dwelled in the forest, the "Puckwudjinies". The Algonquian tribes of North America named them this, meaning "little vanishing people". "Puck" is a generic of the Algonquin dialect, and the similarity to the Puck or Pookie of the British Fae traditions is quite remarkable. Puck, who we know from Shakespeare's merry wanderer in *A Midsummer Night's Dream*, is undoubtedly derived from the Gothic name "Puke", a generic moniker for minor spirits in the Scandinavian and Teutonic dialects. Puck is comparable with the German name for Goblin, "Spuk", and the Danish word for Ghost "Spook". And further comparisons can be drawn from the Irish "Pooka" and Cornish "Pixie".

The Shaman

I have visited North and South America on numerous occasions, and always had an interest in the indigenous cultures both sides of the hemisphere. Over these past couple of years, I've had the opportunity to learn from two Andean Medicine Men, as well as a wisdom keeper descended from one of the Northern Amerindian First Nation Tribes. I have since been taught by them on multiple occasions, and I shall share some of the knowledge passed on to me here. The native healers and wisdom keepers of the ancient traditions of the Andes and the jungles of Peru have a deep knowledge of the mystical and the natural medicines of Mother Earth (Pachamama), as well as a cosmic understanding of the nature of reality. In learning about the Hanan Pacha (the realm of Spirit, represented by the Condor), the Kay Pacha (the physical realm, represented by the Puma), and the Ukhu Pacha (the realm of consciousness, represented by the Serpent), I realized there were many similarities between Amerindian Perspectivism, and the ancient Celtic Pagan tales from my own upbringing in the British Isles. Scandinavian folklore, African and Asian indigenous cultures and indeed more around the world, all share similarities when it comes to our connection with the Earth and the Spirit World. The Ancient Peruvians believed that thousands and thousands of years ago, Seven Seeds were spread across the world, after the Four Elements rescued the planet from a highly advanced race who were plundering the Earth's resources, just like we are doing now. These seeds were strategically placed around the Earth by the "Cosmic Gardeners", so as to give rise to the nomadic cultures and folklores who share demic similarities. Until the year 2012, humanity stayed humble, and mostly lived in accordance with the land and the Four Elements. This has been documented with symbolic writings throughout the cultures of most Amerindian Tribes. After 2012, it was believed that humanity would enter the New Age, an era of a global awakening, and that every generation from then on would evolve at a more rapid rate than the last, and that a shift in Global Consciousness would take place. Needless to say, that era of prophecy is now.

Amerindian cultures of both the Northern and Southern Hemispheres share the practice of connecting with Nature Spirits through plant ceremonies, just like the ancient Pagans. To bring us up to date with a fact-based ancient spiritual elixir, we shall finish this chapter with a very basic version of a Peruvian Cacao Ceremony, which has become popular in recent times. Peruvian healing methods and spiritual teachings have been passed down through generations over thousands of years. The Cacao Ceremony has become a fashionable, healthy and safe alternative to intense hallucinogenic Shamanic journeying involving plants such as seeds of the vilca tree or ayahuasca. The cacao plant increases the brain's serotonin levels, promoting a positive mood, emotional well-being, better sleep, and numerous other benefits. Another feature of cacao is that it helps decalcify, stimulate, and activate the Third Eye Chakra, located between the eyebrows, and our energetic connection to our intuition. During the ceremony, which involves drinking the cacao and meditation (sometimes followed by chanting or singing), the balance between the physical and spiritual aligns, enabling the cacao drinker to connect with their Guides or nearby Nature Spirits. As mentioned before, the Peruvian Realm of Spirit are not depicted as human-like. We all have Animal Guides, regardless of our cultural heritage, and they can be called upon when we are in need of spiritual assistance fairly easily. To address the issue of cultural appropriation, the Cacao Ceremony has been adapted to different cultural beliefs across the world, and the Peruvians themselves have been happy to share their knowledge. Around the early 1990s, the Shamans of South America took heed of their ancient prophesies, and decided it was time to share their 10,000-year-old healing traditions and medicines with the modern world during the time of the Global Awakening. They differ from the Shamans of most Northern Amerindian tribes, who are not typically keen to share their teachings with other cultures.

The examples that I have presented here of the connection between Nature Spirits and Mother Earth are intentionally diverse, and range from the whacky, to ancient and sacred truths. Of course, people have always found medicine in nature. Many people around the world still get their medicine directly from plants, rather than pharmaceutical derivatives. The World Health Organization estimates that 80% of people in the world use some form of traditional remedies instead of modern pharmaceuticals, although this is most likely due to poverty or geographical circumstances. India rates highest, with China, Ghana and Russia close behind. Simply being in nature is a tonic to the body, mind, and soul. Taking a walk through a forest, lying in an open field or besides the ocean, or even just eating your lunch in the park rather than the office, can all increase mental and spiritual well-being. Meditating in a nature-rich environment can help quieten the mind and eliminate unwelcome distractions. Drawing up the Earth's energy with each breath in a visualization exercise is an immensely powerful spiritual practice. But if you can't get to an area of nature, simply adding a ritual to a short meditation at home can be beneficial as well. Lighting a candle or smudging your indoor space prior to meditating can create a state of intention and tranquility. Decorating your apartment with plants can attract Nature Spirits into your home. And who knows, perhaps that favorite tree on your walk to work is actually a Dryad casting a spell on you to remind you to connect with nature.

Exercise: Cacao Ceremony. Level: All Levels

Most mornings, I spend the first few minutes of my day in meditation, with a simple affirmation ritual derived from the Peruvian Cacao Ceremony. I don't chant or sing, although I may sometimes listen to a healing soundtrack or guided meditation. The important thing is to get on with this meditation before the tasks and distractions of the coming day begin. Upon waking, I have experienced being more receptive to Spirit before the thoughts and worries of the mundane crowd my mind. Pay attention to those first impressions you have immediately upon waking. As we come out of deep restorative sleep, our brainwaves enter the Theta state, when we can easily blend with Spirit. This can carry over into our waking state. Don't check your phone if you can help it (I know it's hard), don't turn on the TV or radio. Simply get up, go to the kitchen, and make your cacao drink.

Raw, organic cacao can be purchased at any health food store or easily online. Cacao beans contain essential fatty acids, fiber, minerals, vitamins, phenylethylamine (a chemical in the brain that may improve weight loss, focus and mood), serotonin, and tryptophan. Flavonoids preserve cognitive abilities while we age, lower the risk of developing Alzheimer's, and also decrease the risk of having a stroke. The benefits really are numerous. A tablespoon of pure cacao powder has the same amount of magnesium as a bag of spinach leaves. I have replaced my morning coffee and I even skip breakfast in favor of a drink of cacao and a short meditation. Raw cacao can be bitter, so feel free to sweeten it with a healthy alternative to sugar such as agave.

*Please note, this short ritual is derived from a traditional Cacao Ceremony, and does not attempt to mimic or replace one.

1. Mix your cacao powder with a milk of your choice.
2. Be conscious of the process while your attention grows sharper after waking, concentrate on the action of blending the cacao with the milk and pouring it into a glass while your increasingly-awakening state blends with the day's energies. You can also incorporate this focus into all preparation ceremonies. Making and eating meals is a celebration, and should be treated as such.
3. Take a seat somewhere that you won't be disturbed. Sit in the silence, holding your cup with both hands and your feet planted firmly on the floor. Pay attention to your breath.
4. Send out a note of thanks to the new day. Bless the sky, bless the Earth, bless the sea. Invite your Spirit Guides to come close to you for the day. Thank them in advance and

let them know that you accept all the wisdom they may bestow upon you. Bless all of those who you love and also your extended Earth family including all people, animals and the natural environment. Ask to be of service to all who you encounter today.

5. Bring the cup up to your chest, pausing at the Heart Chakra before bringing it to your lips. Consciously drink the cacao milk, sending out positive affirmations for the day.

6. Once you are finished, take a few deep breaths, and go about your business for the day ahead.

If you are new to this practice, I invite you to take note of how your days progress a week after implementing this morning ritual into your life. I have personally noticed a new increase in productivity, focus, and connection to my Guides. I have also become aware of the manifestation process moving faster and smoother. And hey, last but not least, you get to have chocolate for breakfast!

Chapter Nine: The Dawn of Female Mysticism, Witchcraft, and the Left and Right Paths

Before we turn our attention back to the continued development of our intuition, let's take a moment and look at the heritage of the esoteric as we know it today. To do so, we'll briefly go back to the very beginnings of mysticism, and in turn the origins of mediumship. No matter if you consider yourself to be a healer, an empath, a shaman, a psychic, or a medium, back in the day, you'd have been called a witch.

In Babylonian literature, the decline of the Mesopotamian (modern-day Iraq, Kuwait, Turkey and Syria) female mystics, who were involved in therapeutic healing and ritualistic activities, becomes glaringly apparent during the course of the Second Millennium BCE. These mystical women were highly respected, but a shift took place, where they began to become marginalized, demonized, and in some cases, sexualized. The male cultic officials of the time began to develop increasingly hostile attitudes towards them. These same males were often the scribes responsible for passing esoteric knowledge on to future generations. Throughout this literature, the roles of the Goddesses who were worshipped at the time became replaced by the Gods, and the same happened with women who possessed esoteric knowledge. Healing had traditionally been the territory of women, but the healing arts began to be attributed to male physicians and exorcists. When we get to the biblical era, the role of the female mystic is all but vaguely hinted at, and seriously frowned upon.

You shall not permit a sorceress to live.
– Exodus 22:18

Fast forward to the end of the 12th century, when talk of the spiritual experienced a resurgence in Medieval Europe. Women were once again pioneers of the spiritual practice, and led the search for truth through connection to the All That Is. At the core of this short-lived movement was the idea of the mystical experience being seen as a path towards wisdom. Through the writings of Cistercian monks and nuns, the old traditions began to be reinterpreted with a new flair and zenith. This became more prevalent as these writings began to be written not only in Latin, but in the living local languages of the time. This was a revolution that put into words the personal quest to understand what takes place when one explores consciousness, and begins to point others towards a path of spiritual enlightenment. With this new style, the literature began to favor the secularization, democratization, and feminization of mysticism, and introduced new concepts and expressions that would go on to form the basis of what we now know as modern Western philosophy. As I already mentioned, some of the first authors of this vernacular mysticism were nuns, and also Beguines (similar to nuns but women who took personal, informal vows of chastity, rather than those dictated by the Church). Towards the end of the 1200s, they set in motion a new genre: a mysticism of love that drew on the same sources as what was known as the troubadour literature of the time (a metaphysical, intellectual, poetic style of written word). This style of mysticism evolved into a more speculative kind, based on an innate sense of knowing rather than the rhetoric of religion, much the same as how we now experience mediumship and spirituality. It had its basis in Christianity yet went beyond the confines of the Church, and explored the notion of the self being connected with the Divine, the All That Is, in an ever-fluid cycle of birth, death, and rebirth. Beautiful, right?

The Church didn't think so.

Around the same time, monasteries began experiencing problems with their faithful inhabitants. Monks began reporting that during the night, they were being visited by succubi while sleeping, resulting in overly pleasant dreams. Not only that, in Double Monasteries, occupied by both nuns and monks, the nuns were mysteriously falling pregnant despite abstaining from sex. So the Church surmised that this was clearly something to do with the free-thinking Beguines and their heterodoxic romantic views of the Divine; independent thinking women who claimed to have a connection to the Almighty outside of the doctrines of the Church. It certainly wasn't the monks getting the nuns pregnant, it was clearly the work of the devil. But what about there being no women in the all-male monasteries? How were the Beguines responsible for the monks waking in a sweaty mess if they weren't even there? No problem! It was obviously Beelzebub himself appearing as a wild and wayward woman to tempt the straight-edged monks from their holy duties with unclean dreams and fantasies.

Marguerite Porete was a French-speaking Beguine and mystic, and she wrote *The Mirror of Simple Souls*, a book about what she called the highest form of love, the love of God for the human race and of the human race for God. This resulted in her being burnt at the stake by the Church for heresy in Paris in 1310. She'd refused to remove her book from circulation or recant her views, so the Church decreed the obvious thing to do was to torch her. But the whisperings of courtly mysticism continued, and so did the sordid dreams of monks and the mysterious formation of babies in virgin nuns. So another leap in logic concluded that demons wanted to produce hybrid offspring. Inspired by the new era of predominantly female mystics, these demon succubi would haunt monastic dormitories and steal the human seed from innocent monks to impregnate the heretic nuns and Beguines. And thus the old, ugly, outcast image of the witch from the Old Testament stepped forth from the shadows.

According to the UK Parliament's current website, Witchcraft is the perceived ability to "summon evil spirits and demons to do harm to others", and "was linked to religion to the extent that the medieval church had the powers to punish those who dabbled in magic and sorcery." And like poor Marguerite Porete, punish them they did.

In 1542, the English Parliament approved the Witchcraft Act, which was punishable by death. It was briefly repealed and then restored in 1562, and by 1604 the trials of witches were transferred from the Church to the ordinary courts of justice. Witch-hunting became a popular hobby in the UK and across Europe, and by 1717, approximately 30,000-80,000 witches are believed to have been executed worldwide (including the women and men accused and executed in the famous Salem Witch Trials in colonial Massachusetts). By this time, the witch had evolved into what we recognize as the standard model of the modern era. Crooked, hard, grotesque, a hater of humanity and a converser with the dead. She was able to fool young men into seeing her as a beautiful seductress so she could have her wicked way with them, and she hid in plain sight with familiars to do her biddings. Familiars would typically be a bewitched cat or other housebound animal. It could even be a fly. The witch would feed the familiar and it would grudgingly carry out the appointed tasks the witch would give it. It might also be known as a Brownie or a Hob. Remember those? They enjoy drinking milk and if you spot one naked and offer it clothes, it'll make your life a royal pain by turning into a poltergeist and flinging things at you.

There were also rules to follow. If you suspected that the old village hag or indeed even the hot single thirty-something with two cats was a witch, you had a few tricks at your disposal to keep her at bay. First and foremost, never let her in your house. Or her cat. Or her fly. You could mark the entrances to your home (doors, windows, fireplace) with your own protective boundary spells, such as the five-pointed star, or an M for the Virgin Mary. You must also never let her give you anything, especially not food, and never, ever let her have the last word of a conversation. Next you would need to plead a case to your local authority of the suspected necromancer. If you noticed one of the girls in the village was heading off into the woods on a nightly basis, you could probably assume she was up to no good. Especially if you saw her at midnight. Especially if it was All Hallows' Eve. If enough people had seen her then the poor girl would have no defence, and she would be beheaded or burnt at the stake. End of discussion. By 1735, the UK Government decided that they'd had enough of freelance Witch Hunters, and banned them under the *new* Witchcraft Act. Times were changing, and instead of surmising that witches were real and fornicators with the devil, the new law declared that witches had probably never been real in the first place, and anyone claiming that they had magical powers or talked to the dead were simply charlatans and thieves extorting money from the gullible public. Mediums were included under this new category.

The last witch executed in the British Isles was known as Janet Horne (not her real name, but a generic name for witches in the north of Scotland at the time). She was showing signs of senile dementia, and her daughter had deformed hands and feet. On this basis, and with some very nasty slandering from their neighbors, they were both sentenced to be burned at the stake. Her daughter escaped, but Janet was stripped, smeared with tar, and burned alive. The Witchcraft Act was eventually repealed in 1951.

Let me just say that again.

1951.

That's only thirty-two years before the Internet was invented.

As for the witches of today, they tend to fall in to two categories. Those who follow what is known as the Right Hand Path, and those few who follow the Left. The term originates from Sanskrit across orthodox and heterodox practices of Hinduism, Buddhism, Sikhism and Jainism. Typically, the path of the Right is concerned with seeking enlightenment through connection with the Higher Self, and practicing an ethical code of conduct pertaining to the greater good of life on Earth, much like the Spiritualist code which many mediums abide by. The Left Hand Path ironically owes its nature to the previously mentioned ignorance of the ancients, and is predominantly male, ego-driven, and interested in breaking taboos. It is invested in methods of shock tactics, as well as liberation through sex and substance abuse in order to achieve antinomianism and a self-revered status. It can be argued that all human beings have a dark side, and to face the abyss is to become liberated and set free from the constraints of the ego, what the psychiatrist and psychoanalyst Carl Gustav Jung termed the "shadow self", the uncivilized, primitive side of our nature. He believed that we needed to embrace our dark sides if we were to become fully integrated and healthy human beings. But there is a difference between facing your shadow self, in order to forgive your past mistakes and growing into a better person, and embracing it simply for the sake of living with abandon.

It should be noted here that not all Wiccans identify as a witch. Wicca honors the Divine in the forms of the Triple Goddess, whose aspects of Virgin, Mother, and the Wise Woman are connected to the waxing, full, and waning cycles of the moon. Most Wiccans believe that to experience the Divine is to experience both female and male energies. They are only concerned with the Right Path, or to actively do good for one's fellow humans, animals, the planet, and oneself. "An ye harm none, do what ye will."

There are elements of our human behavior that are good and bad, dark and light. But as with all the practices that we shall discuss in connecting with the Higher Realms, it is our intention which creates our reality, and in wrapping up this chapter, I will remind you that we shall only ever intend to bring the light.

Chapter Ten: Astral Projection and Evidence of the Esoteric

One of my earliest childhood memories is of gliding weightless down the carpeted stairs in our council house in a place called Sinfin, Derby, UK. I remember bouncing lightly on each step, and floating to the bottom. Is this a real memory? It certainly seems so, since it was something I recalled for years before ever discovering the term "astral projection", in a bookstore as a teenager. As I stood browsing through the book, unable to afford it, some of the things written in it rang true with me, so I decided to put them into practice at home that night. I lay on my back in bed, I concentrated really hard on getting up without actually getting up, and eventually I separated from my physical body. I was suddenly in three places at once. I was still laying on the bed, conscious but in a deep state of relaxation. I was floating weightless above my body, and could feel the delicious sensation of flying, the same as it felt in dreams, and somehow I was viewing all of what was going on from the side of the room. I didn't experience myself being at the side of the room, but I had a remote view. It was all too overwhelming, and I snapped out of it. I opened my eyes and jumped out of bed, bringing my awareness fully back to the physical.

Astral travel, an out of the body experience (OBE), or extra-corporeal experience (ECE) are a few other names for this particular ecsomatic event. The latter being a current scientific label which dismantles a supernatural element and puts the experience down to the brain's body schema.

I recently spoke with two friends who claim to have experienced astral travel, both from very different walks of life.

Taina is a Brazilian model and actor, who lives in London. We've worked together a few times, and one of our conversations turned to talk of the esoteric. Taina recounted how the first time she experienced conscious awareness located outside of the body, she was lying in bed with her then boyfriend. She could suddenly see the two of them from a vantage point at the top of the room, as she felt herself shift into two places at once. She went on to tell me that she has since travelled beyond the constraints of the physical world and to other realms and dimensions. The latter is something that I believe we shall explore in Book Three, if I am to acknowledge the subtle nudge I just received while writing that.

Gerard hails from Catalonia, and currently lives in Iceland. We worked together while I lived in Helsinki, and we've been in touch ever since. During meditation at home, Gerard found himself on an airplane, looking at his brother and sister-in-law seated in the window aisle. He noted how they were dressed, what they were drinking, and which row they were seated in. He tried to call his brother when he came out of the meditation. His brother's phone was off, because he was on a plane. When they eventually connected, Gerard's brother confirmed that he and his wife had indeed been on a flight, how they were both dressed, what row they were in, and what they were drinking during the trip. Some years later, Gerard was unable to attend his grandfather's funeral due to work commitments. So through meditation, he intentionally projected his awareness from Iceland to the ceremony in Catalan, and stood in the church besides his mother. When the time came for the burial, Gerard told me how he watched remotely with the other mourners outside in the church grounds. And then something very interesting happened. Another being, not human, was standing beside the burial plot, and looked directly at Gerard. Although he didn't sense any malice from this being, who he had difficulty describing when we spoke, the being gave him the impression that he shouldn't have been there in astral form. After watching the completion of the ceremony, Gerard took the guidance and returned his awareness to his physical form in Iceland. When he later spoke to his mother that same day, she confirmed what he had witnessed by describing the clothes she had worn and the order of the events during the ceremony.

I have always been fascinated with this phenomenon, and have recently begun practicing it again myself. It is not unlike people describing the moment of physical death, often on hospital operating tables, when they talk of a tunnel and a light and reconnecting with lost loved ones before being brought back to life in the physical world. My own mother once described this to me. She told me that when she gave birth to me, a very difficult birth where we both nearly lost our lives, she recalled a warm, welcoming tunnel of glowing green light, and her own mother being there, who she had lost when she was only eleven years old. My mom never talked of anything else supernatural ever occurring during her lifetime, and I never really knew what her views were on esoteric subjects. She told me about this experience very matter-of-factly. I do not doubt that it happened at all.

But others do. Particularly scientists. Despite thousands of people describing similar experiences, regardless of their personal beliefs or religious backgrounds, there are a community of scientists who are opposed to the idea that anything mystical is occurring at all. Mostly, they attribute these phenomena to dissociative disorder, or an inability to recognize body schema. Dr. Susan Blackmore, cognitive scientist, lecturer, author, and psychologist, pretty much disagrees with everything I've ever written concerning consciousness. She had an out of body experience when she was head of the Society for Psychical Research at Oxford University. She goes into great detail describing the event in both her books and subsequent interviews available on the Internet. It prompted her to take a PhD in parapsychology and she spent five years conducting hundreds of experiments on clairvoyance, telepathy, and astral projection. She grew frustrated with a lack of hard scientific evidence on any of these subjects, and gradually went from believing in mystical experiences to an absolute nonbeliever. She says that the reason people often report having a view from above the body during an ecsomatic event is because that view is the easiest for the mind to assemble. She conducted an experiment on a group of students, asking them to close their eyes and picture the room they were in from different angles. Most of them agreed that it was simplest to do so by imagining looking down from a space above themselves, rather than another vantage point such as the floor or corner of the room. Blackmore claims it to be a question of cognitive simplicity, the easiest view to construct, rather than consciousness actually leaving the body. And she's not alone. Professors Andra Smith and Claude Messier, from the University of Ottawa, Canada, conducted an experiment in 2014 to find evidence supporting what they term "extra-corporeal experiences" being real. They deemed their findings inconclusive based on the test being a single case study and the participants' experiences being subjective. They did, however, attribute the phenomena to imagination and hallucinations. They likened the experience of astral projection to an amputee still feeling a missing limb.

As far as science is concerned, an event or experience isn't real until it is objectively proven. A subjective experience isn't scientific fact. Given that the experiences we talk of in these pages are deeply subjective, it will no doubt always remain the same for decades to come. When I have witnessed paranormal events, or felt the presence of Spirit, it tends to not be remembered in the same way as I remember mundane and physical events (as we discussed in Part One of this book). But at the time, the so-called supernatural event is always, always accompanied by an unmistakable sense of knowing. When you experience it, you know it's real (although in the early days, your logical mind might argue that it's not). Furthermore, trying to explain to anyone else what you personally went through is often a losing battle. I'm not particularly concerned about that anymore. I have witnessed enough to know that the esoteric realities I have observed are undeniable. I no longer need to convince anyone else to validate these events. It doesn't matter. And some people are so rigidly stuck to their practical beliefs that they won't budge anyway.

But back to the subject of astral travel. It isn't entirely dismissed within the skeptical scientific community. Studies regarding how the brain reacts during astral projection have found activation within the parts of the brain that govern movement and imagery projection, while the physical body remains still. Researchers observed a subject's brain while the person claimed to be astrally projecting, and successfully identified the unique parts of it that were active during the perceived journey through the astral plane, which reacted the same as when a person is in physical motion. This shows that astral projection is a real experience for the astral traveller.

There is also evidence that points to the validity of astral travel from the US Government's admission that they employed remote viewing techniques during the 1970s and 80s. I'm edging on conspiracy territory here, which is of no interest to me at all, but since this evidence is in the public domain, I shall briefly mention it. A declassified CIA document, released in 2001, talks of something called Project Center Lane. In June 1983, Army Commander Wayne M. McDonnell was given an assignment to assess the psychic services provided by the Monroe Institute, located in the Blue Ridge Mountains, Virginia. He spent a week undergoing their psychic focused treatments, designed to expand a person's consciousness. His twenty-nine page document (available by request from the CIA's website) features detailed description of astral travel, and the conclusion that "intuitional insights of not only personal but of a practical and professional nature would seem to be within the bounds of reasonable expectations." McDonnell included diagrams that suggest consciousness is an intersection of energy planes that exist as part of a hologram, enabling travel through spacetime into the past and future.

Before we attempt astral projection for ourselves, we'll cover a few of the benefits that have been reported from achieving this state. Many people describe how after the experience, they ascend to a new threshold of understanding through a cognitive shift in their awareness. Similar to how people respond to NDEs, or when astronauts return to Earth after seeing it from beyond its gravitational confines. People make career changes, develop a new compassion for all living beings, they begin to respect their own physical bodies more, lose their fear of death, and can also heal grief. It is possible to meet our loved ones who have passed over on the astral planes. During the time away from your body, you may be able to access the multiverse, experience past lives, fly beyond the Milky Way, or have interdimensional experiences. For example, you may witness a blending of your immediate astral environment (your bedroom, garden, or street) with one from the past, including people who lived on that spot before you.

You may or may not have an astral projection experience through following the instructions in the next exercise. If you are someone who suffers with insomnia, sleep paralysis, or lucid dreaming, it is likely you will. It is likely you already have. Suffering from insomnia or sleep paralysis can actually speed up the process of astral travel, rather than being a hindrance. If you don't successfully achieve separation on the first few attempts, perseverance will in time bring results.

There is nothing to fear. It's natural to feel some apprehension in stepping into the unknown for the first time. But here's the thing: To come back, all you have to do is think about your body, and you will be back. Instantly. In fact, I would advise you not to think about your body for as long as you want the experience to last. You will be pulled back there in the blink of an eye the moment you do.

Don't attempt to travel when you are overtired, hungover, or in a negative frame of mind. Use what we have learnt through meditation to assist you in stepping beyond your thoughts. Try to recall any childhood memories or dreams that fit the description of astral projection, they may help.

You can record the following exercise as a guided meditation, but there will be things I want to explain along the way, and for this reason, it would be advisable to read the instructions through a few times, and then attempt the steps in a relaxed state from memory.

Meditation Exercise: Light as a Feather. Level: Intermediate

1. Lay or sit in a comfortable position on a chair, bed, or the floor. You don't want to be too comfortable though, since we are going to attempt to hack the Theta state and remain awake. Theta waves occur in the brain when we are drifting off to sleep or are suspended in that light phase of sleep, just before we wake up. It is the state in which we are susceptible to hypnosis, or are able to practice past life regression and journeying. It's the state where we are able to connect with our Spirit Guides, or you may hear your name being spoken or pick up other voices as though they are on an old transistor radio. It is something we will explore later on in this book. Feel free

to use a blanket to cover yourself. Stretch your legs out, let your feet fall to the sides. Let your arms rest at your sides or interlace your fingers across your belly. Now take a deep breath, and on the inhale, gently expand your stomach as you breathe, and imagine the air filling your belly. This prevents you from taking in short breaths, or that feeling that you can't quite grasp the last bit of air when you breathe deeply.

2. Make any final adjustments you need in order to feel reasonably comfortable. If you end up nodding off to sleep then it's absolutely fine. You must need it. But we're going to attempt to reach the crest of sleep, and then project ourselves beyond the body. Take another deep breath, expanding your belly and letting it fill with air. Do this a couple of times and let your breathing return to normal.

3. Now I want you to set your intention. Reach out to the Higher Realms, your Higher Self, your Spirit Guides, and in your mind's eye, ask for assistance. "I call upon my Spirit Guides, the Higher Realms, my ancestors, to help me in moving beyond the body and to the astral realms, for the purpose of gaining knowledge and understanding of ultimate reality."

4. Now, I want you to scan your body from toe to head. You are going to tense a body part, and then relax it. If you have any physical injuries or discomfort anywhere, skip that body part and just let your attention move over it as we progress. First of all, squeeze your toes tight, and hold for two or three seconds. Then move on to your calves. Point your toes out and feel the calf muscle contract. Hold for two or three seconds, and relax. Next move to your knees. Tense, hold, relax. Your thighs. Tense, hold, relax. Your buttocks, tense, hold, and relax. Move your awareness

up to your belly and your chest, tense them both at the same time, hold, and relax. Move up to your shoulders, lift them to your ears and tense, hold them there, then relax. Now move your focus down your arms and to your hands. Make fists and tense your entire arm. Hold for two or three seconds, and then relax. Now scrunch up your face, make the tightest face you can muster, hold for three seconds, and then relax. Bring your attention back to your breath.

5. Begin to take note of what's behind your eyelids. Are there any swirling colors or lights? Are there any sounds in your immediate environment? Take note of them but attach no significance to them. There is only the moment of now. Anything that is external to you has already moved on. There's no sense in letting your attention follow it. Start to notice your own body again. Think for a moment on the muscles beneath your skin. Feel how warm and soft they are after tensing and releasing them. Feel them sitting relaxed in your current place on the planet.

6. Now I want you to think about your bones. Your skeleton is keeping everything together in your physical being. Visualize it. See your own skeleton protecting all of your organs, holding your muscles in place, and shielding your brain and your heart. Begin to visualize your blood flow moving through your entire body. Little streams flowing tirelessly to keep you warm and alive, all flowing through your heart.

7. Bring your attention to your heartbeat. It's been beating your entire life. It's a constant rhythm that has been passed down to you through eternity from your ancestors. They passed it to your great-grandparents, who in turn passed it to their children. They then passed it to your parents, and your mother passed her heartbeat on to you.

You carry it now. A sacred rhythm carrying a millennia of knowledge from generations that stretch back to the beginning of time. Your heartbeat began at the beginning of time. Feel its rhythm now, beating for you and for this life you currently inhabit. This heartbeat beats so you can do your very best with this life. Your ancestral lineage survived in order for you to be here now.

8. Begin to expand your heartbeat across your chest, feel it move down into your stomach with each beat, then visualize it passing down through your groin, down your thighs, past your knees, through your calves, down to your toes. Once it has hit your toes feel it travelling back up, propagating like a wave, back up through your calves, your knees, your thighs, your groin, your stomach, through your chest, up through the neck and to the top of your head. Now like a pinball it's going to go back down again. Like a laser-scan. Back down through your head, down your neck, through your chest and arms, through your groin, your thighs, your knees, your calves, your feet, and then it's bouncing back again, slightly increasing in speed. Up past your knees, your stomach, your chest, your head, and back down again. Past your chest, your groin, your knees, your feet, and back up. Continue with this heartbeat wave, travelling up and down your body. You may feel yourself begin to tingle and vibrate. Go with it. This is the initial stage of detachment, and while you are doing so imagine that wave rising slightly from your body, pulsating outwards up and beyond your body.

9. Feel your vibrational energy rise with the pulsing wave, feel yourself become weightless as your essence expands up and above you. You may also now decide to flip yourself from the body, imagine turning over very sharply to the

side and out. Visualize yourself peeling away to the side and out of the body's confines.

10. It may take some time to achieve success with this exercise. If on the first few attempts you don't astrally project, bring yourself back by slowing down the pulsating wave, concentrate once again on your heartbeat, then your breath, and open your eyes.

Chapter Eleven: The Tarot

For all of the mystery and suspicion around the card deck known as the Tarot, it started its beginnings in very humble fashion, as a simple card game similar to Bridge. Known as the Tarocchi in 15th century Italy, it went unconnected to the occult for almost four centuries, until the Frenchman Jean-Baptiste Alliette published the first guide to using the Tarocchi for divination purposes. Under the pseudonym Etteilla, he released his own deck alongside the book, with new illustrations and meanings for each of the cards, incorporating beliefs about astronomy and the four elements. He claimed to have been influenced by the *Book of Thoth*, an Egyptian text that was said to have been written by Thoth, the Egyptian God of Wisdom. There are of course disputes around its origins and influences, but with the arrival of Etteilla's deck, the mystical Tarot was born. Etteilla assigned new spreads for the cards, and the idea that the meanings changed depending on whether the cards were drawn upright or reversed.

This short chapter will serve as a rudimentary introduction to the very basics of using Tarot cards. When we return to developing our intuition later in this book, the Tarot can be used as a popular alchemic hereditament of the past, setting us up for the work of mediumship to come.

Many practitioners of cartomancy believe in the presence of Spirit Guides and Guardian Angels. While a Tarot Reader may not identify themselves as a medium, they believe the Tarot to be a direct channel between themselves and their Guides. Through previously studying the cards and also relying on their own intuition, they then go on to interpret the cards for a client, and advise them accordingly on the spread that has been drawn.

There are seventy-eight cards in the deck. Twenty-two are known as Major Arcana cards and fifty-six are Minor Arcana. The Major Arcana represent nature and infinite possibilities, and the Minor Arcana are concerned with our everyday lives. All twos in Tarot cards represent a choice to be made, and all eights mean good luck. Queens represent females over fifteen, and Kings males over thirty. Knights represent young men between the ages of fifteen and twenty-nine, and all Pages are children from birth to fifteen of any gender. Horoscope signs correspond with twelve of the Major Arcana, and Cups, Wands, Swords and Pentacles represent the four elements and seasons. They are also interpreted as human physical features. For example, Pentacles mean dark hair. Swords are dark hair, dark skin, and dark eyes. Wands mean light skin, fair or red hair, and blue or green eyes. And Cups are blue to hazel eyes, with light to brown hair.

Legend says that a person must gift you a deck of Tarot cards in order for them to work. There are a lot of do's and don'ts that Tarot readers enjoy enforcing. It adds to the reverence for the cards, as well as keeping the mysticism surrounding them alive and well. I say go and find your own. Browse your local bookstore or crystal shop. Find a deck that's style speaks to you. I have the traditional Rider Waite deck, published in 1909 and synonymous with the symbols most recognized as the modern-day Tarot. But there are endless varieties released by authors frequently. If the Tarot interests you, find a design that resonates with you, that calls to you, and take it home.

For the purpose of expanding our awareness using the Tarot as a tool, I shall include three exercises. The first will be an intuition-based exercise. The second is a visualization meditation, and the third will be a simple traditional Tarot Card spread. If you don't have a deck or Tarot cards don't interest you, then the visualization exercise can still be performed with a favorite picture, comic strip, or painting. It's not a requisite to purchase the Tarot, but they can be a useful conduit as we get to know our Guides through Part Three of this book. Skip the first and third exercises if you don't own a deck, and concentrate on the second.

Exercise: The Intuit. Level: Beginner

If you are a seasoned cartomancer, you will be very familiar with this simple divination practice of choosing a single card as a meditation for the day. If you have only recently purchased your first Tarot deck, this can be used as a starting point to get to know your cards and an introduction to using them for insight.

1. First take a moment to be still. Concentrate on your breathing and quieten the mind as we have done in all of our previous exercises.
2. Shuffle the deck. You don't have to display Las Vegas-like skills. Just gently jumble the pack, all the while pouring your thoughts and feelings into them while concentrating on a subject you wish to receive insight on. It could be an issue you need to make a decision about, it could be a relationship problem, or simply a subtle guide for the day ahead.
3. Pose your question in your mind or ask it out loud, and pick a card from anywhere in the pack. Let your intuition step in and guide you to the card.
4. Set the card aside and reflect on it. What is the initial impression the card gives you? It doesn't have to correspond with the meaning your Tarot guidebook suggests, although that may still give you some insight. Wait until you look up its meaning. Rather go with your own impression. Does anything immediately spring to

mind? What's the first thing that you thought of when you turned the card? How does the image make you feel? Don't worry at this stage if the card appeared upside down. Concentrate on the colors, the symbol, and the art surrounding the main focal point of the card. Take your impression and address it to your question.

Exercise: Putting You in the Picture.
Level: Intermediate

Pick a Tarot card that resonates with you, something beautiful that makes you feel at ease. If you're feeling adventurous, use the previous exercise and pick one at random. If you don't own a deck, find a picture including a landscape that pleases you. It can be a postcard, a comic strip, or a painting mounted on a wall. Photographs of landscapes can be used at a push, but I would advise against it. Especially not photos including family members or ones that evoke past emotions. We need inanimate subjects that are rich in color, and with places to explore, because that's exactly what we are going to do.

1. Make yourself comfortable. Place your chosen image on a table in front of you and sit on a chair. If you have decided on a painting on the wall, sit where you can see it clearly and are not distracted. You can also lay in bed for this exercise, and place your card or picture on the nightstand beside you. Concentrate on your breathing. Keep your eyes open for now, and ground yourself while feeling relaxed.

2. Glance at your picture. Don't stare at it. Just notice it from time to time and let your eyes wander around the room, all the while relaxing. When you happen to look at your picture again, notice what you enjoy about

it, your favorite colors or brushstrokes, the landscape beyond the main focal point, before letting your eyes drift away again. After a few minutes of doing this, close your eyes.

3. With your eyes still closed, shrink yourself down to the same size as your picture, like Alice in Wonderland after she drank the potion that enabled her to go into the Queen of Heart's garden. Once you have shrunk down, in your mind's eye, get up from your resting place and walk over to your card, and climb into the frame. If your picture is a painting mounted on the wall, glide up to it. If it's on your nightstand beside your bed, hop over and climb on in.

4. Take a moment to survey your new surroundings. You are inside the work of art. Everything is appropriate and proportionate to your new size. Walk around the main focal point of your picture since it is now 3-Dimensional, in fact everything is. Explore the surrounding landscape. Is there a road in your picture? Run down it! Are there trees? Walk around them. Touch them. Embrace the colors and enjoy being immersed in this wonderful land of rich imagination. Take as much time as you like to look around.

5. When you want to return, climb out of the picture the same way you went in. Float back down from the frame on the wall, jump back from the nightstand to your bed, walk across the table to your chair. Return and blend with your physical resting position, and grow back to normal size.

6. Take a few deep breaths. Feel the bed or chair beneath you, wiggle your fingers and toes. Open your eyes and take in the room. Welcome back.

Exercise: Three Card Spread. Level: All

1. Shuffle your Tarot deck while meditating on a question. This spread can be used for a multitude of situations. You are going to draw three cards from the deck after pouring your energy into it and concentrating on your question.
2. From left to right, place your cards face up.
3. Depending on your question, the first card may represent the past, and show you insight into that. The middle card may represent the present, and the third the future.
4. Take your time with the initial impressions you get from each card before looking up their meanings. Doing this will connect you to your own higher truth and intuition.
5. This spread may be used to gain insight into other situations. For example, the first card may represent the subconscious, the middle the conscious, the third the superconscious. Or what you are not aware of, what you are aware of, and the higher insight. With relationships, the first card represents the self, the second the other, and the third the composite energies. With some creativity, the three card spread can be used in numerous ways to gain insight on any given situation.

Chapter Twelve: Things That Go Bump in the Night

In the couple of years prior to my mother's physical death, she would often complain about hearing a knocking sound downstairs in her house, in the early hours before dawn. Always at 5am, always waking her from sleep. She assumed it was a local youngster, perhaps wandering home drunk from a club, and trying the front door. It bothered me that someone was possibly harassing her, and when I occasionally stayed over, I always slept lightly and was ready to accost whoever was intruding on her privacy. It was a safety concern, and she was worried that someone might one day get into the house while she slept. One thing that I never considered (because I had firmly dispelled all thoughts of the supernatural at that point in my life) was that the late night knocking was related to something that had happened during my childhood, years before at the same house.

When I was nine years old, a year or so after my mom had enough of my dad's cruel behavior and took us to a place called Shanklin, on the Isle of Wight, we moved into a house that had just been built on what used to be a kids' playground. I've no idea what it was previous to that. The town's history is linked to the Belgae and Roman Empire, along with the rest of the island. Later on it was used by pirates as a smuggling site, and in the 1800s it was transformed into a holiday destination during the Victorian era. The island is steeped in history, but as for what exactly was on the plot of land where our house was built, I will probably never know. Immediately after moving to the newly-built house, some hinky stuff started going down, and it always happened when I was alone. My mom and stepdad would go out in the evenings a couple of nights a week, and on one of those nights, while I lay in bed reading a comic, a loud bang shook the house, scaring the wits out of me. It appeared to come from the attic, and I hid frozen under the blankets until my parents came home. The banging started happening more frequently, and always when I was alone in the house. Logic would say that it could have been the water tank (located on the upstairs landing) malfunctioning, or "the house settling in", but at nine years old I wasn't big on logic (I still wasn't big on it at forty years old either, but I digress). So the banging continued, rattling the ceiling, vibrating through the furniture, and sometimes there would be two or three in a row. I told the kids about it at school, and suddenly my house was the number one destination for sleepovers. Another night while my parents were out, my friend Neil stayed over, and sure enough, we started hearing movement around the house. This time it went on for half an hour, banging, and then footsteps, which sounded like they stopped right outside my bedroom door. To this day we'll still talk about it, whenever we catch up over social media. I'd decided by that point that the banging and footsteps were obviously supernatural in origin. I told my parents, and as would be expected, they took my concerns lightly. Until one afternoon the three of us were sitting in the living room, and it sounded as though someone dropped a five-hundred pound anvil in the bedroom upstairs. They both jumped up, startled, and ran around the house trying to figure out what had happened while I attempted to point out that I'd been telling them about it for months. Nothing was out of place in the house and the source of the interruption couldn't be found. It went on for years, and everyone began growing used to it, and eventually ignoring it. When I started dabbling with Ouija Boards in my late teens, as mentioned in Book One, the unexplained noises increased. We had a little dog, a Bichon Frise my mom named Tobi, who would sit at the bottom of the stairs, eyes fixated on something at the top. I watched the electric kettle turning itself on and off one Sunday night in the kitchen while I sat doing my homework, and on another occasion an empty can of Diet Pepsi rattled across my bedside table and stopped dead, right next to my head as I lay watching television. And all of this apparent paranormal activity came to an abrupt halt when I'd finally had enough and grown a little freaked out after the Ouija experience. I began practicing visualization exercises with protective auras of white light around both myself and the house. No more banging, no more rattling, no more footsteps. With time I began doubting my memories as my beliefs shifted through various stages of adulthood. Perhaps you have experienced something like this from childhood that you forgot? Perhaps when you grew older you put it down to an overzealous imagination? Obviously, after what I've experienced recently, I'm inclined to believe what I'd originally believed as a kid. The childhood experience that I described also potentially opens the door for further speculation about the grey-haired man on the video call, who I wrote about at length in *Letting Glow*. But my intuition tells me he was someone showing up for my mom, rather than a latent resident entity of the house who hadn't made much of a peep in thirty years other than the odd knock. At the time of writing, I still have the house for perhaps another month or so. It has given me time to grieve and be with my mom's things, and as I sit here now (I've been spending my time between our flat in London, and the island house) it's almost as though I've gotten to hold on to her a little while longer, in a strange kind of way. All of the furniture she acquired over the years surrounds me, the entire house is decorated with her own hands. It's comforting to be here, but somewhat upsetting also. It has been my home since I was a child, and it breaks my heart to have to let it go. Letting it go, is going to be one of the hardest things I shall experience, of that I have no doubt. It has been a beacon to me wherever I was in the world, and soon it shall be turned off.

But alas, practicalities, finances, and work dictate that I have to say goodbye to it.

In the last weeks I have spent a lot of time here on my own, sorting through my mom's remaining things and packing stuff up (an emotional rollercoaster that I document on the *Letting Glow* YouTube Channel, @lettingglowthebook). On more than one occasion, I've been awoken during the night by a knocking sound coming from downstairs, at 5am. It isn't the front door. It's coming from inside the house. And another night, while drifting off to sleep, a loud bang in the attic shook the whole place. That's the first time I've heard it in decades. I don't detect anything of malice here. But I wonder, in exploring mediumship this last year, perhaps I've generated some interest from random veiled entities, or a visit from an old childhood friend.

Chapter Thirteen: Manifesting in the Multiverse of Madness

If you've read *Letting Glow*, you may remember that immediately after my mom passed away, I worked on a major movie production from Disney and Marvel called *Doctor Strange in the Multiverse of Madness*. In the film, and the comic books preceding the film, the hero Dr. Stephen Strange exists in multiple universes as well as our own (or the Marvel Cinematic Universe at least), where he presides as the "Sorcerer Supreme". He is able to manipulate time and reality itself by casting spells learned from his studies at "Kamar-Taj" (I've been there, it's quite impressive), and his magical artefacts and technologies.

As entertaining as the stories of Dr. Strange are, they also tap into deep scientific theories on the nature of time, reality, and consciousness. In order to progress effectively, we won't delve into all of those theories here, nor do I want to be accused of choosing those which reinforce my own beliefs. But the following leads nicely into the next couple of chapters before we return to the world of mediumship with a clearer interpretation of the metaphysical world we inhabit, along with the physical one that we understand.

Famously, in 1935, the Nobel Prize winning Austrian-Irish physicist Erwin Schrödinger came up with the theory that if you placed a cat, and something that could kill the cat (radiation, in this case), in a box and sealed it, you wouldn't know if the cat was dead or alive until you opened the box. So until the box was opened, the cat was in a suspended state of being both dead and alive simultaneously. This represents how scientific theory works. No one knows if any scientific theory is right or wrong until a theory can be tested and proven. Schrödinger's supporters were in agreement that the theoretical cat in the theoretical box with the theoretical poison was indeed in a hybrid state until the box was opened and all statistical probabilities collapsed into one reality: the cat was dead or alive when observed.

In 1957, a young American man named Hugh Everett received his PhD in physics. He considered Schrödinger's cat in a box scenario illogical, and went about proposing a new theory. He agreed that the cat existed in the unopened box, but the fact that it was consciously observed once the box was opened, bore little significance on whether it would be found to be alive or dead. He suggested that both realities existed together, and that when the box is opened, the conscious observer actually splits into two realities; one observer views the cat as dead, while the other identical version of the observer views the cat as alive. Then each version of the observer goes off to write up their report on the cat. One where the cat lives, one where it croaked. Those two realities veer off in different directions and in turn create multiple upon multiple realities from their significant points, causing a ripple effect where two different universes create their own futures. But Everett's Many Worlds Interpretation (MWI) goes beyond a cat in a box. His proposal implies that if the theory works, then this fractionation would have already taken place at the moment of the Big Bang, at the dawn of time as we so far understand it, causing alternative splits upon splits at the quantum level, meaning that all possible scenarios of all events have happened and will happen in an ever-expanding universe.

Phew!

So with this theory, every possible outcome of every single event is taking place simultaneously in trillions and trillions of universes that are each splitting into more universes that continue to split and expand forever. And needless to say we are part of this continued expansion, meaning that there are multiple yous living in multiple outcomes based on multiple decisions that those multiple yous have made and continue to make. And we haven't even got to your parents and the decisions that they made! Or your grandparents and ancestors. It's mind-bending.

Professor Stephen Hawking expanded upon this and presented a complex mathematical theory called "the observer created universe". He suggested that each universe doesn't branch off and continue independently to the others, but rather exists simultaneously in a state of superposition, waiting to be observed. So each and every universe is in an ever-changing state of limbo waiting for each and every version of us to make a decision. When we do, the universe that contains the outcome of that decision collapses, leaving all the other universes in a state of superposition, and so on. This ultimately means that you are constantly creating your own universe, *manifesting* your life into existence, and so is every other version of you out there in the multiverse. Each decision that you make brings a new outcome in every reality, meaning the potential outcome of every decision is already there, suspended in a state of superposition, waiting for you to choose it, *whether you choose it or not.*

So in a way, the "vision boarders" may have been on to something, whether they understood it at the parallel universe level or not. We are each creating our own reality, we are each building upon our thoughts and intentions by putting them into action at a conscious level. There is *so much more* to our reality and we are only just scratching the surface of comprehending it. The mystical and metaphysical need not be separated from science or be at opposing views. As we've already discussed in the previous chapters, our understanding of the natural world has evolved from believing in Faeries and mermaids in the Middle Ages, to thought breeding creation in a multiverse of possibilities. The person in the Middle Ages that danced around a well inhabited by an Undine, while carrying a chicken, was essentially setting their intention and choosing the desired outcome from a multiverse of outcomes. They just probably didn't need the chicken. Sleeping with a daisy under your pillow and willing your lost lover to return is suggesting an intention in a universe of possibilities, you're simply focusing on the possibility that you desire. A witch, bestowing a curse upon a villager was merely suggesting an alternative future that the villager could either reinforce with worry, or cast aside as nonsense and choose a better outcome from an infinite amount of outcomes, suspended in a state of superposition waiting to be chosen. Taking the Left Path or the Right, saying positive affirmations aloud or declaring them on social media to friends. You are setting the intention for a desired reality. Tapping in to your childhood awareness through meditation and refocusing on your dreams is making a decision to connect with the alternate reality where you became what you always wanted to become. It's never too late to change direction. It's still out there, just waiting for you to find it in a parallel universe.

Intention is everything.

Part Three: The Developing Medium

Chapter Fourteen: Nanyehi

This final section of the book will be dedicated to establishing a connection with the Higher Realms, our Spirit Guides, and those who we have lost. We shall also return to our overall quest of developing our intuition and connecting with deeper truths.

I don't claim to be a professional medium. I'm not even sure that I want to be one. Other mediums repeatedly tell me that it's my destiny, ever since I first stepped inside a Spiritualist Church. But I don't currently sit with clients, attempting to connect them with their lost loved ones. I don't ask for money to perform demonstrations online or in person. I don't call myself a Spiritualist either, nor am I affiliated with or a member of any associations, unions, or missions (although I have studied with the Spiritualist Association of Great Britain and the London College of Psychic Studies). But one thing I am certain of, and at some deep, deep level always have been, is my connection with Spirit. It had already begun way before I lost my mom. From astral projection as a child, to a shift in the perception of time as an adult. Every couple of years something new would show up, something unexplained, radical, and something that I would usually dismiss thanks to a lifetime of cultivating a rational mind. I was awoken one morning by my Spirit Guides, when I experienced a downloading of information through the Crown Chakra (I had no idea what a Spirit Guide or Crown Chakra was at the time). I didn't know what was going on, but I knew that something light years beyond my own intelligence was attempting to give me a mass of information. I panicked. I felt overwhelmed.

"Do you still want this?" they asked. It was as though I'd already agreed to receive whatever information it was they wanted to give me. But I had no recollection of it. I sat bolt

upright in bed and begged for it to stop, and it did, leaving me dazed and looking at a holographic grid all around me, which faded out and eventually disappeared. In hindsight, it was as though they were perhaps preparing me for what was to come. It seems I was already being guided to this path years before my mom passed, and as you know by now, her passing was the catalyst for me beginning to walk it.

A traditional Spiritualist might not endorse what I'm doing here. It takes years of practice for most people to become mediums. Gordon Smith, arguably Britain's best, told me that he practiced for seven years before he ever did a reading. So did James Van Praagh. I'm not going to teach you how to set up a business as a practicing medium. I wouldn't know how to do that. But I am going to share what I have already learned so far about connecting with the Higher Realms, because it seems that's what the Higher Realms want me to do. We are going to do this through fine-tuning our intuition, and we're going to do it together. I'm practicing as you're practicing. I may be further ahead or behind you on this journey. It doesn't matter. I know that what I'm writing here will get us to where we want to go. I know because so far, it's working.

I'm still getting to know them, those Guides who abruptly woke me one morning. They've been quiet for most of this book. I can only assume that they weren't interested in talk of witches and government projects or Tarot card spreads. They only seem to step in when the time is right and the subject pertains to the bigger picture. I believe they'll be joining us again for this last section of the book.

Occasionally, I'll see one. In moments of meditation, in workshops, in dreams, sometimes just randomly throughout the day. Later on, we're going to talk about how you can meet your own team of Guides too. You may have even met them already, whether you were aware of it or not. Let me tell you about something that happened only yesterday.

I already mentioned that I have studied with Shamans from both North and South America. The Amazonian Shamans of the South have recently become very liberal with sharing their millennia of knowledge with the rest of the world, since they believe the time has come to do so. The Native Amerindian tribes of North America still mostly keep their teachings fiercely guarded, with a few exceptions. I've always had a lifelong fascination with both the North and South American Indigenous peoples, and over the years I've explored the ruins of Tulum in Mexico, and taken countless trips to Florida, North Carolina, and other States time and time again through my twenties and beyond. I've always felt at home there, I felt drawn there. Always there. I was even looking into the legalities of obtaining a visa to live there at one point, but opted to return to my native England instead, after twenty years of living away from it.

When I was sorting through some of my things at my mom's house recently (the time grows ever closer to having to let that house go, which is breaking my heart) I came across a series of books buried at the back of a closet on North Amerindian Shamanism. I'd bought these books years ago in my early twenties when I visited a Seminole Reservation in the year 2000. (Traditionally, Northern Amerindian knowledge was only ever passed down verbally, and never to non-natives. There is a venomous online presence rejecting any Native American authors of Amerindian Spiritualism marketed to the wider world. In fact it is so immediate in denouncing all authors who share this knowledge as frauds, that it's suspicious.) I'd never really gotten around to reading them, and had completely forgotten about their existence until now. I remember enjoying the idea of what the books represented, but I never understood what the teachings actually meant. I'd soon given up on them after reading only a chapter or two, and as I leafed through them recently, I was astonished at how closely the teachings in these books mirrored what I've been learning as a developing medium. There was even a section on time being nonlinear. If I would have read that all those years ago, I'd have perhaps comprehended what happened to me later on with a lot more clarity.

So I packed up these books and brought them back to London with me. Yesterday, I sat on the balcony of our London flat and did a midday meditation. I mixed up a glass of pure cacao powder with milk and turned the meditation into a short affirmation ceremony. I lifted my awareness to the Higher Realms while setting my intentions for the week ahead. I asked my Guides to come close, as I usually do, and somewhere during the stillness, I saw a beautiful Native American girl. She presented herself at around twenty-five years old, and she was dressed in traditional clothing. Then she was gone, just as quickly as she had arrived. I wondered if she'd been a figment of my imagination. I had, after all, been reading the books I'd brought back with me, along with a new book on Amerindian cultures. I'd incorporated a Peruvian Cacao Ceremony into the meditation, so maybe it was no wonder that I was seeing visions of Native Americans. I didn't think too much of it. I took note of it, and went about the rest of my day.

Later in the evening, I wandered down the road to Barnes Healing Church. I hadn't been in months, and thought I should go and say hello. It was one of the first places I'd gone after losing my mom, when the medium Janet Neville had given me a message from her. When I arrived last night, there were a handful of people chatting in the back room. One of them was a medium I hadn't met before, an older gentleman dressed smartly in a suit and tie, and as the evening went on, he started doing a reading for me. In fact we all got one, since there were only five or six of us there, and immediately he started talking about Florida.

"I feel a deep connection with Southern America," he said. "Not Peru," he added immediately, interestingly. "But the South Atlantic States, like Florida. Would that make sense to you?"

"Actually it would," I replied, being careful not to give him any more information than was necessary.

"Do you have any connections there?" he asked.

His question was more loaded than he realized. I of course have friends there, people I've met through my travels over the years. But I also have a deeper connection, one which I haven't told many people. My grandmother on my father's side had met an American soldier in World War Two when he was deployed by the US Army to the UK to help the English fight the Germans. I don't know anything of the affair, only that my dad was the result of it, and his mother gave him up for adoption soon after he was born. The story that I was told, was that every year, my dad would receive a birthday present from Florida, all throughout his early childhood, and when he was old enough to travel alone, my dad flew to America to track down his own biological father. He found him, and his name was Ed. I know nothing more of the story since the last time I spoke to my dad was when I was eighteen, and that was a long time ago. I only know that Ed was married and had kids, and he had asked my dad not to visit him again.

"You have twelve eyes on you," the medium said to me. "You have six of your Guides around you right now."

He paused.

"Would you have any American Indian heritage in your bloodline?" he asked.

I said that I didn't believe so, but I didn't tell him how very fascinating I found the question since my renewed interest in Amerindian cultures had recently resurfaced.

"There's a beautiful young Native American lady with you," he said. "She has high cheekbones and long dark hair. I think you know this already."

"I believe we met today," I said to him, never failing to be amazed at how often these readings were spot on. "But I wasn't sure if I was making her up."

"She's one of your Guides," he told me. "There may be an ancestral heritage there. Your Guides are telling me that you have a powerful voice for Spirit, and that you will be instructing people on how to find their own. Does that make sense?"

"It does," I replied. "More than you'd know."

We wrapped up the reading and I thanked him for the insight. When I went home in the evening, I looked up traditional Amerindian female names and found one that resonated. I very quickly offered it to my newly discovered Guide. Nanyehi. It is a female Cherokee warrior name meaning Spirit Person. She immediately appeared, in an instant, and offered me a bright yellow sunflower.

You are going to meet at least one of your Guides through reading this book. It might not be tomorrow, but if you implement the teachings here it will happen. We can't force it, and they will come when the time is right, but we shall learn how to recognize the subtle energies and hints that they are there. When the time comes, you will know. But before we meet our Guides, we will first learn how to sense our loved ones who have passed over. I have connected with my mom many times since she has passed. I recognize when she is near, and we don't need our Guides when we connect with those who were very close. First we will start with meditation practices and raising our vibration, and then we shall reach out. You will learn to differentiate between your imagination and a real connection. Trust the process. Let's glow.

Chapter Fifteen: Theta. The Receiving State.

This chapter is for those of us who have recently lost someone. We'll start simple, and we'll start with the familiar.

Grief shows up in many ways. I'm sure, by now, that you have dreamt of your loved one in Spirit plenty of times. It can be of great comfort, sometimes followed by a great sadness upon waking. Particularly in the early days. I don't believe that grief will ever cease. As of writing, it has been seventeen months almost to the day since my mother passed from this life to the next. I have found solace in exploring spirituality in all of its aspects and through my adventures into mediumship. Great solace, in fact, since I have connected with her many times both through my own practices and through other mediums. But in the very earliest days, she would come to me in dreams.

At the beginning of this book, I told you about the very personal experience of the day I lost my mother. I expanded on what I've written previously, and recounted what happened the night following her death. As you may recall, I believe that she shared her moment of transition with me from this world to the next. I stood with her in a room full of swirling colors, while she checked on me that I was going to be alright before she crossed over. It was so very vivid and real, and I've never had a dream before it or afterwards in such technicolored veracity. It was heartbreaking and beautiful. And not, surprisingly, uncommon.

As mentioned at the beginning of this book, the *American Journal of Hospice & Palliative Medicine* says that, "Anecdotal evidence suggests that some loved ones and caregivers of dying patients undergo a type of end-of-life phenomena known as a shared death experience or SDE, whereby one feels that one has participated in a dying person's transition to a post-mortem existence." They conducted a content analysis report of 164 SDEs, that revealed four distinct though nonexclusive modes of an SDE: remotely sensing a death from a location far away, witnessing unusual phenomena, such as seeing the dying person's "spirit" leave the body at the moment of death, feelings of accompanying the dying, and feelings of assisting the dying.

Dr. Raymond Moody, philosopher, psychiatrist, author and firm believer in life after death, talks about the shared death experience in many of his books and television interviews. "As the person in the bed passes away, the bystanders have experiences that are identical to those that are reported to us by those who are resuscitated after almost dying."

In my personal experience, I didn't know of this phenomena until researching it afterwards. To address the issue of the amount of time that had passed between my mother's physical death earlier the same day and me having the experience later that night, I believe that time is irrelative between our world and the Higher Realms. I believe that is why I had the experience some years ago of time being nonlinear, in order for me to prepare for learning what we are learning now. This is something that we'll explore further, later in this section of the book.

She was just here, as I wrote this. Right now. I smelled her perfume and so I stopped writing, closed my eyes, and listened. We talked of that moment and my current day-to-day dilemmas. I thanked her for coming by, and I got back to writing.

And so on to the subject of connecting with our loved ones through dreams. You can have your own sleep connection with a loved one in Spirit that doesn't have to be as profound as the one I described above. They visit us all the time when we dream, since our brain is alternating between the Theta and Delta wave states. Theta waves occur when we're drifting off to sleep or are suspended in that light phase of sleep, just before we wake up. It is the state in which we are susceptible to hypnosis, or are able to practice past life regression and journeying. Both Delta and Theta waves occur when we sleep, but Delta waves are the ones that dominate periods of the deep, restorative kind. In essence, when we are in the Theta state, we are in a passive "receiving" state where our intuition can pick up subtle energies without any effort, right before the prefrontal cortex of the brain (the part that distinguishes between thoughts and decisions) can catch up and start questioning everything. During the Theta state, you may have already experienced hearing your name being spoken by a family relative or friend, right before you fall asleep. Or you may have heard voices that sounded like they were coming from a radio when you wake up.

The following exercise is a simple one to establish an initial connection with your loved one in Spirit. If you have recently lost someone, this is the first step towards reconnection, since when we are in a deep pocket of grief, it can be hard to still the mind and remain open. This exercise cuts out the need to actively attempt a calm and open state, which is often difficult to do when you are in the thick of it. You can make it into a larger ritual, such as lighting a candle before bed and signifying your intention of connection while holding something that belonged to your loved one, but it isn't necessary. Simply go to bed with a clear head, try and put aside any worries of the day just lived or the one on the horizon, and begin to think of your loved one as you drift to sleep. They will immediately be with you, whether you recognize their presence or not. So take comfort in the fact that your intention alone will draw them close.

Meditation Exercise: Sleep Meditation. Level: All

Record this exercise as a guided sleep meditation. Leave a few seconds of silence between each verse. It can be used over and over again, and whenever you have difficulty falling asleep. When you climb into bed and turn out the lights, play it through comfortable headphones with the volume low, and try not to concentrate on the words too much. Just let your mind wander and let the instruction guide you to sleep. Don't voice the numbers, just move to the next instruction in a calm and relaxed manner.

1. As you go deep into relaxation, your body feels heavy, and your mind reaches for the void that is sleep. Your body is about to recharge itself, your mind too, and it's time to let go of any worries or problems from the day. Take one deep breath, and on the exhale feel the worries drift away, like a white feather floating on the breeze.
2. Think of your loved one. Recall their eyes filled with love when they looked at you, imagine the smell of their perfume or the scent from their clean clothes. Remember the timbre of their voice that was uniquely theirs. No one else sounded like them. Hear them in your mind now and let it comfort you. Think of words of wisdom they offered you or might offer you now. Remember their laughter and the fun you both had in each other's company.
3. Recall the times you spent together. Think of holidays, meals in restaurants, birthdays, and days at the beach. Let the memories come from all times. Perhaps you were a young child, perhaps it was only last month. It doesn't matter. Let the good memories come and let them overlap and change and go from one to the next and back again. Don't force them, just let them flow and feel what they bring to you.
4. Your subconscious mind is now doing all the work for you. Your mind is growing still, reaching for the peaceful, warm, encompassing void. Feel your loved one's hand, soft and warm in your own hand as you walk side by side and into sleep.

5. Let's count now from three to one. When we get to one you will let yourself go deeper and deeper into relaxation. Let your mind just drift to the next level. Let it go on a lovely journey to reconnect with your loved one. A wonderful peaceful walk with your loved one on the Spirit Plane. Three, letting go. Two, letting go and connecting even more. And one, deeply relaxed.

6. It's OK if your mind wants to just sleep now, just let it go. Three, feeling light. Two, going down deeper into sleep. One, sleep and let it go.

7. Let any sounds you might hear take you even deeper. If my voice begins to fade that's absolutely fine. You're going deeper now, and your loved one is going deeper with you. Let any movements you make take you even deeper. Let any thoughts you have just come and go, fading like distant memories. Fading away. Three, two, one.

8. There's a path in front of you. A peaceful path through a beautiful forest bathed in sunshine and lined with flowers. As you walk this path, you notice that where your feet would normally hit the ground, instead they're floating just above it. You are floating above this gentle path that leads you to one of your favorite places. Almost as though you are on a moving escalator that takes you to that peaceful place you want to go.

9. Three, going deeper and deeper. Two, you're feeling so good and relaxed now, the more relaxed you feel the deeper you go. One, falling asleep.

10. Your loved one is beside you, floating along the path as you go forward hand in hand. Three, you are arriving at a clearing, and your special place. Your loved one is smiling beside you. Two, you are going deeper into sleep now, and totally relaxed. Every time you listen to this you will go deeper quicker and longer. One, you are in deep sleep

now, sleeping the whole night through with your loved one holding you close.

11. There's a hot air balloon waiting in the clearing for you. You walk over and you climb in to the basket together. You are feeling so relaxed and happy, and you're both having so much fun. The balloon begins to drift upwards, and you feel it leaving the ground. As you move above the canopy of trees you feel weightless and free. The experience feels so restful and pleasing as you float higher and higher and leave the world below. The air becomes fresher and cleaner, and all worries are escaping through the top of your head and out into the sky as you connect even more with your loved one besides you.

12. As we count down now you are fully immersed in sleep, and these words hang suspended in the background as you drift away and into the sky. Three, you are connected with Spirit and your loved one is talking besides you. Two, you are completely relaxed and loved. One, you are in a deep, restful, restorative sleep.

Chapter Sixteen: The Art of Listening

Everything speaks. Don't worry if you can't hear, because all you need to do is listen.

A few years ago, I moved to what is currently the third busiest city in the world. London is behind only Mexico City and New Delhi, in terms of a mass population. New York or LA don't even break the top twenty. It's very, very difficult, to find a spot in London where there isn't someone already. Even my beloved Richmond Park usually has a person somewhere, wandering across a field in the distance sooner or later. If you've ever been to the wilderness, without human contact for days, the surprise at seeing someone else's world behind a stranger's eyes can have a jarring effect on what you thought was a solitary moment. When I first moved to London, I found it exciting, in fact I still do, six years on. The buzz of people, the bars, the restaurants, the concerts and plays, the opportunities. There's always, always something to do here, and you could do something for the first time every day of the year for the rest of your life if you chose to. So it's kind of ironic that I found the practice of meditation, and going into the silence, for the first time in my life since moving here. Or maybe it actually makes sense. Because we all need a break from other people from time to time.

When we're lucky enough to sit beside an ocean, we enjoy the calming sound of the waves. Whether they are gently lapping on the shore or during the roar of a storm, something speaks to us directly from nature. It retunes our senses and connects us to the environment and ourselves. We become revitalized. We feel part of the natural world. To use a current buzzword, it "re-wilds" us. Eventually, the sound of the waves turns into white noise, and we get lost in our thoughts. The sea's an easy one. We can physically hear it. But what about looking up at the night sky on a quiet night, in your back garden or a country field? What about when there's no lapping of the waves, but only silence?

If you've ever stood before a mountain, have you heard it speak to you? If you've ever witnessed the grandeur of a row of mountain summits, or a hill range, have you heard what they have to say? One of my teachers, the Andean Medicine man Puma Quispe, told me a story of when he was walking with his grandfather. Puma began training with his grandfather, the late Shaman Don Maximo Quispe, after an initiation by lightning at the age of six, and he learned to master traditional Andean rituals by connecting with Ancestral Spirits, cosmic forces, and natural Elementals. He said that one day, while trekking far from his village of Chinchero, in Peru, he and his grandfather stood on a hillside and looked in wonder at the mountains across the valley. Puma, only a young boy at the time, told his grandfather excitedly that he wanted to climb those mountains, but they were at least two days' hike away.

"Go there," his grandfather told him.

"How?" asked Puma, confused.

"Close your eyes, listen, and go there," Don Maximo said.

Everything speaks. Don't worry if you can't hear, because all you need to do is listen.

Have you ever stood before a giant oak tree, perhaps in a forest or park, and heard what it can tell you? I visit my favorite tree in Richmond Park at least once a week. I make the time to go there, I take a bottle of water with me, and I go and sit on the hillside beside it and tell it my latest woes. I place one hand on its bark, and breathe. I spray its trunk with the water, in a symbol of respect and an offering of thanks for the wisdom I receive. And I always receive wisdom. Every time. We sit together and I meditate, and I quiet the mental chatter of my monkey brain and find the silence. And I listen.

Have you ever been sitting on a bus, or on a busy subway train, or inching along slowly in traffic, and the whole journey is driving you nuts because you have somewhere to be, and it's hot and stuffy and you are constantly getting distracted by this person or that car, or you're listening to a podcast or the radio and all the while you know you're going to be late for work and there's a million things you need to do that day and you'll never have time to get them done? Of course you have. But you have an opportunity to find the silence right there. Even with someone breathing down your neck fifty feet below street level, or with the air-con not working in the car while you're stuck on the highway, or while the plane sits on the tarmac delayed for another hour. See the mountain, listen, and go there. There is a keen difference between listening and hearing. We can listen, but never hear. We've all experienced talking to someone who didn't hear what we said. Likewise, we've all been guilty of zoning out mid-conversation. The same is true when we go within. We should be present and able to listen to both the heard and the unheard.

If we are to connect with Spirit we need to learn to go "into the silence", or to "sit in the power", or whatever you want to call it. There are multiple opportunities to connect to it throughout the day. If only for a moment. If only for just one breath. By learning to quiet the mind we learn to recognize our thoughts, and by learning to recognize our thoughts we are able to detach from them. By detaching from them we are able to dance in the space between them and observe them. And by observing them we learn to recognize the difference between our thoughts and our intuition. And eventually, when we connect with Spirit, we learn to recognize the difference between our own thoughts and intuition, and the messages we receive.

Chapter Seventeen: Orangutans and Sweetcorn

Most books that focus on the subject of mediumship tend to fill their pages with direct accounts of readings for clients. I've read a few of these books, and when I was going through the initial stages of grief, found some solace in them. My intention with this series of books is to avoid overly recounting moments of mediumship. I don't need to try and convince you that mediumship is real by force-feeding you the time that "this" happened or the time that I witnessed a medium saying "that". I would rather share my own journey of exploration and hold the door open for yours. But in doing the latter, I suppose it's inevitable that these stories must be told. Indeed, I have a vague plan to end this book with one of those stories. There is also something to be said for the first few times when, as a developing medium, you pass information on to someone else that they validate to be accurate. And what I am about to tell you is a lesson in learning to trust your intuition and not second guessing what you see. It's all too easy to think that you're making it up, particularly as we are new to this.

I recently attended a workshop hosted by the medium Gordon Smith, and he paired me up with a young lady I'd never met before who was from Canada. I don't remember her name now, only that she was in her mid-twenties and polite. If you choose to explore mediumship further than this book, workshops can help you progress in leaps and bounds, and are a great booster to any development circle you might already be involved with. They take you away from your regular teaching environment and give you the opportunity to practice with a completely new group of people that you know nothing about, making the validation process much clearer when the time comes to practice. In this particular class led by Gordon, we had already been through a meditation exercise designed to open us up to Spirit and connect us with our Guides, and we were each put in pairs. I went first, and attempted to tell my Canadian partner something that I was receiving from Spirit that I couldn't have possibly known otherwise. I took a few deep breaths, and tried to see the space between my thoughts, because that's where it's at. That's where everything's at.

"I'm seeing an elderly lady," I told her. "She's in a nursing home, and it's her birthday." That was exactly what I'd seen. An old lady sitting beside a window, she was surrounded by birthday cards and balloons. She looked incredibly sad, and rightly or wrongly, I made the decision not to convey this to my partner.

"I can take that," she told me, following the rule not to give any information that might lead me in any way.

"I'm feeling grandmother," I said, although it seemed an obvious estimation. My practicing client confirmed that her grandma on her mother's side was in Spirit. I asked my Guides to give me something else and went back to that place between the thoughts. I felt their presence, right behind me and over my left shoulder, which is where they'd recently begun to make themselves known.

"I see a yacht, cutting through blue water," I said now, telling her exactly what I was seeing. "Good times, friends. People are partying. It's summer and you're carefree and are about to receive important news." I looked to my partner for confirmation that I wasn't just making stuff up. She watched me for a moment before answering.

"Last summer," she said. "Well, should I tell you? I don't want to give you too much information."

"I think I'm nearly done," I replied, sensing that this was all I was going to get for this girl. I still needed to ask for a message.

I went back to her grandma. "She's saying that she missed you, but that everything's fine now. She's fine." I pressed for more. Please give me something else. "Or that it couldn't be helped," I added. "Does that make sense?" I should note here that this particular workshop was around the first year mark of me practicing mediumship. I knew that I was done. I didn't expect to get a name or anything more than I'd already given.

"We were on our yacht with my friends when she passed," she told me. "On her birthday."

I received a small jolt of surprise and pride that I'd gotten it right. And then reminded myself to take me out of the equation. I hadn't gotten it right. I'd asked my Guides and they'd facilitated the meeting between myself and this young woman's grandmother. Not only that, there was absolutely no reason for my pride to swell because none of this had anything to do with me. We were talking about her family, this person who I had never met before. This wasn't about me being right or wrong. I was simply the go-between. The medium.

"Thank you," she told me. "Shall I try now?"

"Please," I said. It was her turn to try and connect me with someone in the Spirit World. I watched her as she closed her eyes and within seconds she started telling me what she could see.

"A rural place," she said. "Corn, sweetcorn. Does that make sense?"

I thought of the Isle of Wight, where I grew up, and where my mom lived the rest of her days. Sweetcorn is one of its main produce and I'd even had a stint picking it for work when I was a teenager. I didn't otherwise have any affiliation with sweetcorn though, and thought it to be a pretty strange suggestion. If she was talking about the Isle of Wight then maybe something like beaches or the sea would have clarified it to me better than sweetcorn.

"Sure," I said. "I can sort of take it. It's not anything that's really connected to me though, but it might make sense."

"Alright," she replied, eyes still closed and going deeper. "Dresses. In this rural place. Does that make sense? I'm seeing ladies' dresses with floral patterns. Long-flowing summer skirts with pretty flowers. Rows of these dresses."

OK, there was no doubt about it being the Isle of Wight now. For weeks, well, ever since my mother had passed, I'd been visiting her house on the island and sitting in her room staring at her cupboards full of clothes. Lots of dresses. Lots of floral summer prints. I'd recently given a few to a local lady to make into a patchwork cushion for a keepsake, but I was still finding it incredibly hard to let go of the rest. In fact, as I write now, they're still hanging in those closets. I find it difficult to let go of them. They smell of her perfume. But I know that it has to be done.

"OK, that makes sense," I told her.

"Who's got the cat?" she suddenly asked.

"Erm, yeah, I mean I've got a cat," I said, talking about Määtä, Laura's Finnish cat of fourteen years who we had flown over when we moved to London. From the night my mom passed away that little cat has sat on my chest every single night before I go to sleep. Every night. She did it last night and she'll do it tonight. She never did it before. She waits for me to climb into bed, and then comes and lays on my chest until I nod off.

"This might sound a little odd," she laughed. "But there's a tattoo of your cat?"

Wow. This was accelerating fast now. I'll explain in a moment.

"She's having some fun with me," my partner went on. "She's showing me a photograph now of denim shorts? Like when you'd take a pair of jeans and cut them into shorts. Does that make sense?"

I couldn't help but smile. I couldn't believe my mom would be telling her about the denim shorts.

"Yeah I'm quite sure I can take that," I let out an exaggerated sigh. "I think you've got my mom."

"M-hmm, I think I do. She's telling me to ask you about the shorts," she smiled.

Well great, these two seemed to be getting along just fine. Somewhat at my expense. This was wonderful though, really. No one else knew what she was telling me, other than perhaps my fiancée. Everything she was saying was one hundred percent accurate.

"OK, so you wanna tell me about the denim shorts?" She grinned at me mischievously.

"Alright so firstly, when you talked about sweetcorn, I believe you were talking about the place where I grew up, a place called the Isle of Wight in the south of England. The dresses thing makes sense. I recently lost my mom and for the time being I still have her house on the island. I've been struggling to go through her things even though it's been over a year, and the dresses is a big one for me. And the cat, the cat tattoo's the one that's done it. My mom adored our cat, she absolutely loved her. And in the year before she passed she kept talking about getting a tattoo of the cat's face on her arm."

"Well she's telling me that she's just had it done," she smiled.

"That's lovely," I said, shaking my head and smiling.

"And what about the shorts?"

"Christ. So. The denim shorts. You have to remember I'm considerably older than you. Fashion trends have changed. Sometime in my teens when I didn't have much money, I turned a pair of ripped jeans into shorts one day at the beach. And there's a picture of me wearing them. We had a day out once with my mom and cousins, actually my cousins who I've recently reconnected with since my mom passed, and there's this picture of me wearing them. For some reason my mom framed this awful picture. I'm standing in these shorts with a drink in my hand. She framed it and put it up in my bedroom when I moved out, and it's still sitting there now. In fact it's been there so long that I barely notice it. I still hate it though."

"Well I think your mom's telling me that she's watching what you're doing. She knows you're struggling with letting go of her dresses, and she knows that you're spending time at the house. She sends you her love and is telling you to keep an eye out for a particular floral print."

I thanked her for the message, and we went back to tell Gordon about what we'd experienced.

In one of my other development circles, we would start each session by opening up the main Chakra points. Not everyone does this, and it's not something that I always practice now as I further my development. But in the beginning, it proved a useful visualization tool. One evening during this circle, I was partnered with an older English lady that joined our circle for the first time that night. She was perhaps in her early sixties, and we hadn't said a word to one another until that point. We went through the usual process of connecting with our Guides, and I began to tell her what I saw.

"An elderly gentleman," I said. "Sitting in a high-backed chair. He's almost bald on top, and he reminds me of the actor Robert Duvall."

"Sounds like my father," she said quickly.

"He's telling me..." I paused. What I saw next was weird. If you're as old as me, you might remember that during the 80s there were a bunch of posters that had tacky slogans on them. There was a famous one with a lady on a tennis court, there were also shirtless male models shot in soft monochrome, holding babies and staring at them wistfully. And there were monkeys. Lots of monkeys. Particularly Orangutans. Particularly baby ones, usually doing something silly and usually accompanied by a slogan that said "oh shit" or something like that. Well that's what I saw now. One of those posters with a baby Orangutan and a slogan. This Robert Duvall-looking gentleman was letting me know that he was keeping an eye on things. And what he was keeping an eye on was baby Orangutans. This was about as bizarre as it gets.

"OK, this is going to sound weird," I started. Our teacher Gilly, who was leading the circle, encouraged me to go on. "I'm seeing a baby Orangutan? In a nappy. Like a diaper." The few people in the group murmured with hushed laugher. I thought I'd obviously made a mistake. But there it was. I silently asked my Guides if what they were giving me was correct. I imagined a blank screen, and wiped it clean. Give me something else on the screen, I thought. Are you sure about this? Again, a baby Orangutan wearing a diaper appeared. Big brown eyes, red hair, cute face.

"Yeah," I said, opening my eyes. "Baby Orangutan."

The lady smiled at me.

"My daughter works at an Orangutan Sanctuary in California," she told me. "I believe what you're trying to say is that my dad's keeping an eye on her."

If I'd have dismissed that and not said it, I'd never have been able to give her the message her father wanted me to tell her. If I'd have ignored the part about sweetcorn when my Canadian partner had been telling me what she saw, it would have perhaps thrown her off and I wouldn't have received such a fun and playful message from my mom. In hindsight, it actually made more sense for my mom to use sweetcorn as a link to make me think of the island rather than the beach or sea. They would have been too vague. I hadn't realized it at the time, but I always connect sweetcorn to the Isle of Wight.

Say what you see. In the early days, it's easy to think that you're making it up. You don't even have to be a developing medium. It might be that you hear your loved one's voice randomly through the day. Out of nowhere you hear your mom's advice. Or you smell your grandma's cooking. Or you hear your friend laughing with you. Or that song on the radio reminds you of them. Don't dismiss it. Go with it. If you are actively seeking a sign, or connecting with Spirit, it's more likely that you have made a connection rather than you're making it up. Trust your instinct. Go *between* the thoughts. Go with the first thing that comes to mind. Open yourself up and trust that what you are doing works.

Chapter Eighteen: The Guides

We already established what Spirit Guides are in *Letting Glow*, and I've talked about them freely here. But to reiterate, a Spirit Guide is essentially the medium between the Spirit World and you. To establish your intuition at its highest level, you need to get to know them.

According to Wikipedia, some Spirit Guides are persons who have lived many former lifetimes, paid their karmic debts, and advanced beyond a need to reincarnate back into this life. Many mediums believe that Spirit Guides are chosen on "the other side" by human beings who are about to incarnate into this life, and are assisted by these chosen Guides throughout their earthbound lifetimes. Spirit Guides can be Animal Guides, Nature Spirits, Star Beings, Ancestral Guides, and other incarnations. I met my own Animal Guide in 2020, prior to diving headlong into mysticism and a full year before writing Book One of this series, and I've met others since.

Spirit Guides are here to inspire us, to direct us, and occasionally to warn us. Some may refer to their input as intuition, that gut feeling which guides us during uncertain situations, and indeed through developing and recognizing our intuition, we shall open the pathway of communication with our Guides. Sometimes their voice is loud and clear, others it's a gentle tug to steer us towards a better version of the future.

Perhaps the most famous psychotherapist of all time, Carl Gustav Jung, talked about Spirit Guides with no hint of irony or suggestion that they were the product of mental imbalance. During Jung's time as a research scientist, he came to the attention of Sigmund Freud, the founder of modern psychoanalyses. The two men corresponded at length, and collaborated on a joint vision of human psychology. Freud saw the younger Jung as the heir he had been seeking to take forward his "new science" of psychoanalysis. But Jung's research and personal vision made it difficult for him to follow his older colleague's doctrine, and the two parted company in 1911. This division resulted in the establishment of Jung's analytical psychology as a comprehensive system separate from psychoanalysis. Among the main concepts of analytical psychology is "individuation", the lifelong psychological process of differentiation of the self out of each individual's conscious and unconscious elements. Jung considered it to be the primary subject of human development. He created some of the best known psychological concepts, including synchronicity, which he used to argue for the existence of the paranormal, archetypal phenomena, reflecting deep cross-cultural metaphysical truths, and what he called the "collective unconscious".

Jung wrote of meeting his Spirit Guides, the most famous being one he named "Philemon". He observed that, "Philemon and other figures of my fantasies brought home to me the crucial insight that there are things in the psyche which I do not produce, but which produce themselves and *have their own life*. Philemon represented a force that was not myself. I held conversations with him, and he *said things which I had not consciously thought*. Psychologically, Philemon represented superior insight." To anyone else, Philemon might have been dismissed as a figment of Jung's imagination, or evidence of madness. But Jung was convinced that Philemon was real, and that Philemon was in the Spirit World and somehow capable of communicating with Jung using his own thoughts and imagination.

So how do we know that when we start hearing voices, that we're not going mad? Typically, schizophrenia, bipolar disorder, psychosis, severe depression, and Alzheimer's generate the hallucinations associated with hearing voices. The key factor in differentiating between connecting with your Spirit Guides or suffering from a mental health disorder is that these diseases are accompanied by other symptoms. Randomly hearing your

Guide advise you to suddenly turn left to avoid a motor vehicle accident doesn't mean you need to see a doctor. And if you are actively seeking out your Guide by following the instructions in this book, chances are those gentle nudges you'll begin to sense, or the images in your head or indeed even voices that you might hear, will be one of your team of Guides.

Recently, I began slacking with my daily meditations and connection with my Guides when other areas of my life began to crowd in. It's inevitable that this happens. When you realize it, you simply have to take the time to realign with your Higher Truth at the earliest convenience. I found myself once again at my mother's house, on the Isle of Wight, dealing with potentially letting the place go, which grows more inevitable as time passes. On this particular afternoon, I found myself musing over my Guides. This was prior to meeting Nanyehi, who I wrote about in Chapter Fourteen. I was in a reflective mood, and calm state of mind. The perfect time to connect with my Guides, I decided. It was early evening in June, and the sun was beginning to set over the houses across the street. I went outside, sat on the front porch, and cleared my mind. I was going to conduct a short test. After a few deep breaths, and attempting to find the space between my thoughts, I sent out a note to my Guides.

"Tell me something about the Isle of Wight, that I don't know," I asked. Immediately, I received a thought that was not my own.

*"*****es Hotel in Shanklin, was used by local prostitutes as a brothel, for passing travellers and highwaymen in the mid-1800s."*

What??! OK, that was very specific, I thought. It definitely wouldn't be something that I would have thought of, nor anything that I would have ever researched otherwise. I immediately whipped out my phone and Googled it. The hotel in question, which I am leaving nameless so as not to upset its current proprietors, was opened in 1857. It definitely would have been used as a stable and rooms for passing travellers. But there was zero information on it being used for the oldest profession.

OK, I thought. Maybe a little too specific. Give me something that I can research. Something about the island that I would never know.

"The bay at Bembridge has a serious algae problem."

Alright then. Bembridge is an area of the island I know very little about. They have a small airfield and a windmill. I know they have beaches. But the entire island is surrounded with beaches so no news there. Algae is something I know nothing about. I know that it's some sort of seaweed, and that's about it. I'm not a fisherman. I've been fishing twice. Once when I was four, with my father, and once when I lived in Finland. I know nothing of marine biology. So this was definitely something about the island that I knew nothing about. I Googled it.

Immediately, I found an article: "The green seaweed saps oxygen from water – meaning other marine life cannot survive – and spreads, taking over hundreds of acres of mudflats and estuaries. The waters around Bembridge are particularly susceptible to this problem since low tides prevent much movement between the coast and mainland."

Good enough for me. I am certain I didn't know that. As much as I love the ocean I've never taken more than a casual interest in marine life. I barely even eat any sea dwelling creatures. I quickly got in touch with a friend of mine who had recently moved to Bembridge, and is an avid fisherman. He confirmed the issue and found it funny that I was asking about the algae problem there, since he knew that I had no interest in such matters.

I thanked my Guides and felt satisfied that they'd answered my questions. I don't advise "testing" your Guides like this regularly. Trust needs to be primary. But in the early days of our practice, asking a specific question can reassure the occasional doubt and reestablish a connection.

When embarking on the path of mediumship, it's important that we get to know our Guides and build a relationship with them. Your Guides are your biggest supporters. They want nothing but your best. They work behind the scenes and help to point us towards our best futures. They interact with others' Guides and orchestrate harmonious outcomes for all parties involved. When you reach out, they rejoice and align with you more clearly. And when you begin to connect with Souls who have passed over to the world of Spirit, your Guides are the ones who make the meetings happen.

It is important to remember, that your Guides work with you, not for you. When connecting with us, you need to find the space between the lines. Dance around the thoughts, as Phillip has so eloquently described. We are your Tribe of Elders, the seekers of your Highest Selves, the custodians of the secrets of your soul's path and heritage, yet you only need to ask to learn. To establish a connection with your Guide is to find your inner truth. We are everywhere and nowhere, we are the breeze whispering in your ear, we are the rustle of leaves in October, we are the birdsong at dawn. In time you shall learn to hear us directly, but it takes perseverance. We are in no hurry, for you truly have all the time in the world. Come then and dance with us, we are your effervescent friends, we are connected to your greatest self, we will never, ever do you harm, for that would be beyond the realms of what is possible nor would we want to. We seek the greater good of all of life, both physical and beyond, and we orchestrate the greater outcome. We are but a thought away.

Effervescent friends. I like that. Beautiful. I don't think I would have come up with that in a million years. So here we go.

Let's take this further now, and I invite you to join me in this meditation to prepare for connecting with your Guides. Record it on your phone and play it back to yourself if you are reading the hardcopy of this work.

Meditation Exercise: Heal and Glow. Level: All

Before we begin to reach out to our Guides, let us get used to raising our energy and sending it out into the world. You may send healing to someone you know who is in a difficult situation, or suffering from an illness. You might want to send your light out to the world to contribute healing to a current global crisis. You may want to send your loving energy to a loved one in Spirit. Either way, this meditation isn't about you. It's about sharing your own source with the other.

1. Sit where you won't be disturbed for ten minutes or so. Have your feet placed neutrally on the floor, with your back as straight as is comfortable.
2. Relax your shoulders and take a couple of controlled deep breaths. As you relax, feel your arms and legs grow heavy, and let your jaw go loose. Let your belly go soft, and as you inhale, expand your belly and visualize filling it with each breath.
3. Imagine now, pulling up the Earth's healing energy through your feet. A soft, golden or green glow travelling up from the Earth's core and directly into your body. With each breath you pull it higher, feeling it travel up through your calves, then your knees, your thighs and your groin, up through your belly, swirling around your chest and down your arms to your fingertips, up through your neck and into your head. It brings healing light to every dark corner of your mind, illuminating it with love and positivity. You feel warm as this light

fills you, warmth traversing the landscape of your physical being.

4. Now focus on your Heart Chakra, spinning about ten inches in front of your chest. As it opens up, I want you to direct your inner healing light through that Chakra, and out into the world. See it expand as it goes out, a sparkling, healing ray of light, and start directing where you want it to go. Is there a person or a place, a difficult situation, that you believe needs healing? Visualize that person, place, or situation, and send the healing light there. See the light enveloping it, like a soft, healing balm, and making the situation, person, or place better.

5. When you feel your work is done, pull the light back towards you. Not bringing any of that situation that you healed back with it. The light is clear, it is pure, it has served its intended purpose and comes back to you with joy and reverence.

6. Bring the healing light back through your Heart Chakra, and as you do close the Heart Chakra like a bud, pulling it back to your chest. Let the light travel back down through your body, through your feet, to be recycled in the Earth's core.

7. Become aware again of your physical surroundings. Wriggle your toes and fingers, take a couple of deep breaths, and open your eyes.

Chapter Nineteen: Animal Guides

Our Animal Guides are perhaps the easiest to meet, and we shall begin with reaching out to them before we connect with the rest of our team. As well as worshipping the Norse Gods, the ancient Shamans of Scandinavia revered their Animal Guides. The Scandic Shamans honored the great eagle, which dwelt upon the branches of the Cosmic Tree "Yggdrasil". It was seen as a symbol of universal nature. Medicine Priests attached plumage and the severed heads of hawks to their shoulders, turning the heads to face them, as though the birds were in conversation with the Shamans. This is often depicted in pictures of the Norse God Odin.

The Native American tribes of North America would embark on Vision Quests to meet their Spirit Guides. They would deplete their body of energy with physical exertion and fasting, and travel to a place in nature where they would not be disturbed. They would then undertake a physical task to further fatigue the body and distract the conscious mind, such as piling rocks. After awhile, they would begin to see wildlife that would become increasingly friendlier. The animals who approached could be accepted as Guides, or the seeker could strive to hold out and thank the Animal Guides who presented themselves, commenting on their strength and beauty, but informing them that the seeker waited for one greater. Eventually, perhaps days later, their main Spirit Guide would appear. They would then take this vision back to their Tribe of Elders, and the vision would be deemed as acceptable or not.

In 2019, I began to feel an inkling of what was to come, and found myself reading a book on Shamanism. This sudden interest was inspired by waking up one morning, seeing a glowing grid above me, while receiving information through the Crown Chakra from my Spirit Guides. But at the time, I didn't know what a Crown Chakra or Spirit Guide was. My mother was still alive, the world hadn't gone through a global pandemic, and I didn't have the slightest idea of associating my esoteric experience with mediumship. But something was making itself known to me, and I felt that a sensible approach to exploring whatever might be going on would be to learn about those ancient tribes associated with the Shaman. I felt drawn to Shamanism. Interestingly enough, I found the answer to what happened to me in the first few pages of the book. A glowing grid was often described as appearing when the Shamans of North America would communicate with their Spirit Guides. I decided that I wanted to meet these Spirit Guides of mine again, since the initial connection had been too overwhelming and had come without warning. The book taught me that it was easiest to meet what was known as an "Animal Guide". So I downloaded a Shamanic drumming soundtrack to my phone, walked into Richmond Park, lay a blanket beside my favorite tree, plugged in my headphones, and entered what is known as the Lower World. The Lower World is the realm of ancestors and spirits. It is based in the natural world and it is the deepest aspect of our Soul. It is a beautiful, earthy dimension, where we can connect with our Animal Guides. Since the beginning of time it has contained nature's secrets which are instinctual to our spiritual growth. It is where the power of the Earth, its elements and its kingdoms can be encountered. Where wisdom as well as power may be brought forward into our embodied existence. Every thought and idea planted and cultivated by humans throughout history are imprinted in the Lower World. Here is where the light within the Earth may be accessed to bring growth as well as healing. It is where I met my Animal Guide, and was taken through memories of childhood and certain instances when my Animal Guide was around to protect and encourage me. These memories came out of nowhere, particular moments when I had been or was about to be physically injured, or times later in life when I needed courage and strength to overcome daunting situations. I was shown that this Guardian had always stepped in, surrounding me with its strength and sometimes fury, yet all the while it sat with me during this vision, indifferent and cool. The experience amazed me. I was also surprised at how easy it had been. I'd met my Animal Guide on the first attempt. I thanked him, and went through the process of closing down the meditation and coming back to our physical world.

I was taught the meanings behind Animal Guides from a descendant of the Cherokee Nation. You may find different meanings associated with different Guides in your own research. Most are common sense and self-explanatory. And it must be noted that respect for ancient customs must be adhered to at all times. Animal Guides are most often associated with the tribes of the Native North Americans. Descendants of these tribes guard their heritage fiercely, hence the practice of usually only passing knowledge through the generations verbally. Their history is entwined with a long and violent colonization that filtered and in some cases altogether halted the practice of their own belief systems. It's no wonder that they keep their teachings so close to them. Doing an online quiz to find your "Spirit Animal" or casually mentioning that cats are your "Spirit Animal" because you like laying around a lot could be construed as the appropriation of the beliefs of Indigenous peoples.

Out of respect for ancient beliefs, I don't practice meeting my Animal Guide on a regular basis. In fact, I have only attempted it twice so far. Both times were successful, and both times I received the information I sought.

All of that being said, we are learning how to meet our Spirit Guides here. I don't believe that Animal Guides are exclusive to one nation or belief system. We are each connected to the

Divine (or whatever name you choose to call it) and no one has an exclusive hotline to the All That Is, or is any better equipped to engage with the Higher Realms than anyone else. That's where the problem with religion arises, and that's where the problem of division arises. Spirit doesn't care which tribe you belong to. Spirit doesn't care about your religious background. But with respect in mind, we shall attempt to connect with our Animal Guide.

Meditation Exercise: Meet Your Animal Guides.
Level: Intermediate

If you are able to get out in nature for this exercise, it would be hugely beneficial. But if not, visualizing somewhere that you enjoy such as a woodland or beach will help also. You'll need an entry point, to what is known in Shamanic terms as the Lower World. The entry point can be a hole in the ground, a door in a tree trunk, a body of water such as a stream or the ocean, a cave, or even a holographic portal. If you haven't met your Animal Guide before, then you won't know what yet to expect. Your Animal Guide has chosen you. You both made an agreement before you came to this world. You won't know which animal they are until they appear. Don't go with any preconceived notions about what you might find. You will also need to set an intention. Don't just show up with nothing to say. Think about an issue that you would like insight on. You'll want to ask your Animal Guide this question when you meet them. Don't ask a question that requires a simple yes or no. Ask about something that needs specific detail. Also, try to avoid asking questions that begin with the word "when", because you are journeying to a place outside of time. If you stick with these guidelines, then when you come back, you'll be more convinced that what just happened, truly happened. Alternatively, you may ask your Animal Guide to perform a healing on you, if you are suffering physically, mentally, or emotionally. If you are able to listen to the soundtrack of a drum through this meditation, by all means do so.

1. Find a comfortable place to sit or lie down. Close your eyes, take a couple of deep breaths, and relax. Place your hands on your belly, and feel the breath vibrating through your physical self.

2. Let your breath return to normal, and think about a place in nature where you have been before. Visualize yourself there. Take in your immediate surroundings. Listen to any sounds that are native to that environment. Enjoy the scents. Feel the ground beneath you. Take a walk around the area in your mind's eye and notice if there is an entry point to the Lower World.

3. Now take in a deep breath again to the count of five. Release the breath to the count of five also. Repeat this a few times.

4. Notice any thoughts, feelings, or energies, that come up as you breathe. Now step back from these thoughts as they come and go, and let your intuition take the reins.

5. Now imagine noticing an opening into the Earth, experience yourself entering the opening. You will find yourself in a place of transition, a tunnel or portal that leads you to the Lower World.

6. Follow the tunnel down, and begin to silently repeat the affirmation that you wish to meet your Animal Guide. As you walk down your tunnel, feel the ground beneath your feet. Is it soft? Hard? Is it made of dirt, grass, or sand? Is it moist or dry? Follow the light up ahead, and emerge into the Lower World.

7. Notice your surroundings. Is it night or day? What kind of plant or animal life is around you? Is it cool or warm? Is it

raining? What color is the sky? Can you even see the sky? Or is there a canopy of trees? Breathe in the fragrances. Know that you are in a place of beauty. Know that you are in a safe space of peace.

8. Look around you. Can you sense a presence nearby? Is your Animal Guide behind you?

9. Once you are aware of this loving Guardian Spirit ask, "Are you my Animal Guide?" If the Light Being who is with you is not in the form of an Animal, then they are another member of your Spirit Team.

10. Thank your Guide for coming to meet you. Now ask your Guide, "What do you have to teach me?" Feel any changes to your being. Is your Guide connecting with you telepathically? Are there any physical sensations? Let your Animal or Spirit Guide share the knowledge they want to bestow upon you.

11. Now is the time to ask your question. You will know the answer instantly. Or ask for healing. Trust your intuition.

12. It's now time to return to your waking state of consciousness. Thank your Guide for the experience, and turn to leave. Retrace your steps back through the tunnel, the same way you came in. You are carrying the knowledge you received there with you back to the waking world.

13. Return your consciousness to your physical self. Wiggle your fingers and toes. Notice any sounds around you and feel the seat or ground beneath you. Welcome back.

Chapter Twenty: Humility (Originally Titled Subatomic)

Hugo Gernsback (1884-1967) was a Luxembourgish-American inventor, writer, editor, and magazine publisher, best known for publishing the very first magazine dedicated solely to science fiction, *Amazing Stories*, in 1926. He also invented the very first version of what were essentially rudimentary noise cancelling headphones, so he could concentrate better while he wrote. But he came to the conclusion that: "Even if supreme quiet reigns, you are your own disturber practically 50% of the time." It seems that we are hardwired to pull ourselves away from what we attempt to concentrate on. Sustained attention on abstract concepts doesn't seem to come easy to us, let alone concentrating on actual work. We like to use the term multitasking. But this was a term invented in the 1960s to describe a computer working on two programs at once. Even a computer shifts its attention to a primary task over others. There seems to be an optimal window when we are able to give 100% of our focus to a project, and according to current science, it's only 90 minutes. After focusing for 90 minutes at optimal levels, our thoughts begin to drift, and we need at least 20 minutes to reboot before starting again.

Many studies have recently been talking about our general attention span, which is different from the task-oriented attention span. According to recent Internet clickbait and newspaper articles, our idle attention span is now less than a goldfish (nine seconds).

So how do we sit still, meditate, and take the time to connect with our Higher Selves or our Guides? Especially if, according to recent polls, the average person looks at their phone one thousand five hundred times a week?

As well as stepping back from our thoughts (which we have covered now ad verbum), the next key is a shift in thinking. We have to begin to truly look at ourselves as "spiritual beings". If you are not yet doing so, I implore you to begin right now. We've already bridged the gaps between living in 3D, 4D, and 5D. You could break those categories down further still to the Non-Believer, the Spiritual Seeker, and the Modern Mystic. By this point into this book, I would expect you to at least identify as a Seeker. It's time to realize that you are a Light Worker, and that you have been called to action. You *are* a "spiritual being" having a temporary physical experience. Spirit is energy. *We* are energy. Physical matter is made of atoms too small to see with the human eye, and each atom holds 0.001% matter. The rest is energy that vibrates and flexes at all times. These countless particles move so fast, that they appear to be solid. To the human eye, we are physical, solid beings. At the subatomic level we are simply multifarious vibrating...

The wind is a wonderful thing.

Erm... excuse me? Would you care to elaborate?

Be wary of becoming too concerned with the ifs and the whys and the maybes. For now it's beyond the limit of human understanding. And it's meant to be that way.

When you feel you can't connect with Spirit, remember the wind is invisible and breath is the direction to connection with the intuition. Always. Focus on your breath. The invisible breath that is in abundance always and everywhere. At any given moment. Always there. Take a breath, an ethereal, glorious breath that connects you to the All That Is, that is forever and always.

Thank you.

I guess I was getting a little caught up in myself there. I'm no expert on this. And I was just reminded that I'm not. I'm tempted to cut this chapter out and start over. But I believe that was invaluable advice that came through right there. Was I getting a little ahead of myself? Maybe. I'm no scientist, I shouldn't be talking about particles and atoms. I probably shouldn't even be talking about goldfish. Nor am I a spiritual guru. I shouldn't be saying that I "expect" anyone to be anywhere on their own personal journey. I'm learning. The point of these books is for us to learn together.

I'll leave this chapter as an exercise in humility. I was just corrected. I was making grasps in the dark and my ego got in the way. I was straying from what I genuinely know and my own experience. I'll return to that now.

Once you have learned to quiet the mind, attaching no preference to the thoughts that come and go, focus on connecting with the Higher Realms. The next thing you want to do, is raise and expand your energy.

Thank you. That's where we shall go next.

Chapter Twenty-One: Raise and Glow

Wow. How amazing was that? My Guides stepped in and literally told me to shut the hell up and stop overcomplicating things.

It's an odd one. I know those parts are not from me. I would be sitting here writing to myself if that were the case. In my opinion, the writing style changes completely. The language grows richer and lyrical. It's kind of amazing to be honest. But it's not me. I don't take the credit for it. I don't even know which Guide it is yet. Perhaps it's one or perhaps they take it in turns. Perhaps they communicate in unison. I begin to feel a tingling sensation, at the back of my head. Sometimes I feel a presence, behind my left shoulder. This happens occasionally in meditation also. But it seems to be the calling card that they're close, and they want my attention. We'll talk more about recognizing when your Guide is near in the next chapter.

Let's get to work.

I hope by now, that the distinctions are clear between connecting with our Spirit Guides and connecting with our loved ones in Spirit. We don't need our Guides to connect with those who were close to us. That bond is unbroken. I feel my mother come close from time to time, without my Guides bringing her near. Likewise, I feel my Guides and recognize the difference in energies. If you eventually end up working as a psychic medium, then your Guides will bring in your querent's friends and family in Spirit. They will be the go-between the two worlds. Your Gatekeeper Guide will organize an orderly queue for the people on the other side who want to communicate with their loved ones in the physical world, through you. When someone passes from this world to the next, it's still possible for them to send signs and nudges to us who still live. But to communicate, Spirit searches for those who are able to bridge the gap between the two worlds, and sustain the energy necessary to keep the connection and communication going. To receive messages from Spirit, we need to raise our energy so that those in the Higher Realms can blend with it. Those in Spirit can hear our positive thoughts. When we think of our loved ones, they know it. When we ask our Guides to come close, they come close. Just the intention of attempting to connect with our Guides draws them close. Don't worry if in the early days, you can't yet feel the blending of your energy with theirs. Don't worry if you can't yet hear their voice. The act of reaching out will draw them near. They know you want to connect, and they shall applaud and embrace you.

So to get us used to inviting our Guides into our personal space, we will do a short meditation exercise to blend our own energy with the realm of Spirit.

Meditation Exercise: Glowing Up. Level: All

1. Sit where you won't be disturbed for ten minutes or so. Have your feet placed neutrally on the floor, with your back as straight as is comfortable.
2. Relax your shoulders and take a couple of controlled deep breaths. As you relax, feel your arms and legs grow heavy, and let your jaw soften.
3. Let your breathing return to normal. Imagine, as you breathe, that you are pulling in pure white energy with each breath. A glowing aura of white light surrounds you, and with each intake of air you pull it deep inside your body.
4. Feel the glowing light travel around your body now, to the tips of your fingers, to your feet, feel it expand in your chest and light up your head. You are glowing from within now, and the light has reached the darkest recesses

of every inch of your physical being. Feel it expanding, as though you are a living, glowing beacon of light, because after all, you are.

5. Imagine raising this shimmering light upwards, just a few inches. Feel your light beginning to rise from your body, a foot or so above your head. Your entire light being has now shifted from your physical self, to just outside it. You are that light.

6. Now clear your mind, and let any thoughts come and go and be on their way. You are going to focus on a single thought now, and that is to invite your Guides to come close and blend with your energy. Just gently ask them to come near, and if there is anything they would like to let you know. Tell them that you are open to receiving their insight. Be open to either consciously or subconsciously receiving any information that your Guides want to share with you. You may not hear it, but you are receiving it at a superconscious level.

7. Continue to breathe in the glowing light and raising it above you. You are breathing in the light of Spirit and it is blending with your own. Get used to sitting in this state and take notice of any subtle differences in the energy around you. You may sense someone close. You may experience a tingling sensation somewhere on your person. You may feel sensations of warmth or cold around you. You may not experience anything, it doesn't matter. Trust that your Guides are reaching out and blending their energy with your own.

8. If there is any sensation that happens to get your attention, ask your Guide to recede it, and see if you feel it move away. Then once the sensation has gone, ask your Guide to bring it back again. You are both gently and purposefully

connecting with each other. Do you sense more than one Guide near you?

9. Thank your Guides for coming close, and for any knowledge they have shared with you. Know that you have received it, even if you didn't perceive it. You can return to this exercise as often as you wish, and in time the connection will grow strong. Ask your Guides to move away from your sacred glow now, and begin to bring your light back towards your body. Let it fill you once again, and then concentrate on bringing it to your center, to your heart.

10. Take a few deep breaths, and become aware of your physical surroundings once again. Feel the chair beneath you, hear the sounds around you, and when you feel ready, open your eyes.

11. Feel free to make a note of anything you experienced during your meditation.

Chapter Twenty-Two: Befriending Your Guides

When you explore the world of Spirit, it seems that everyone and their grandmother has a Native American Spirit Guide. Myself included. If it hadn't been confirmed by the visiting medium at Barnes Healing Church, I may have dismissed my vision of an Amerindian tribeswoman as being influenced by the books I was reading at the time. It's typical to see archetypal figures as our Spirit Guides when we begin reaching out. It's normal to expect and visualize a strong, noble ideal of what we would like our Guides to be. You may very well have Jim Morrison or Marie Antoinette of France as your personal Guide, or it could be that your Guide is presenting themselves in a manner pleasing to you for your initial contact. I have so far met a Panther, briefly glimpsed a floating, extremely joyous-looking Buddha, a Viking-type warrior, and a First Nations tribal woman. One of my Guides claimed to be an old friend of mine, an Ascended Master who I have known in a previous life when he worked as a jeweler in Israel. He came through my circle leader with this information.

When you attempt to make initial contact, I would advise to trust your feelings when reaching out for the first few times. In some of my early meditations to connect with my Guides, I often sensed a cluster of beings, and could see them standing in the distance and edging ever closer. Time will tell if the archetypal images I have received are true representations of my Guides, or if they are presenting themselves as different aspects of my psychological desires. Some of these archetypes (Viking, Amerindian, wise Buddha) are ones that I have shown interest in and learned about at some point in my life. Or then it could be that I showed interest in and learned about those cultures because I have those influencing Guides. This latter point is something to take note of. If you suddenly find yourself drawn to a particular culture or period of history, it might be one of your Guides pointing you towards their direction.

Don't worry too much if you haven't had a vision of your Guide. Trust your feelings first. Take note of how the atmosphere around you changes when you reach out. Notice if there is a sense of someone near when you attempt to make a connection. Do you have any physical sensations? As weird as it sounds, when I started, the muscles in my arms would often twitch as I attempted a Spirit Guide meditation. I would also feel slightly nauseous. I began to recognize these sensations as early indicators that I was on the right path. I don't get either of those feelings anymore. Now I have a tingling at the back of my head, and the sense that someone is behind my left shoulder. I don't necessarily always see anyone appear. I often don't know which Guide is drawing near or influencing me. When you start to recognize that a Guide is close, you can ask for a physical sensation, and see what you get. I have heard of people feeling a tingling on their neck, or a gentle brushing of their cheek. If you don't get anything so obvious, when you sense your Guide is in your space you can ask them to step away from you, and then to come back into your space so that you begin to recognize the subtle difference in energies. Be patient. They are always there.

Many teachers advise their students to take notes. I have to admit, I've been terrible at this. I would occasionally write something on my phone after a meditation if I had witnessed or sensed something particularly profound. Mostly I just trusted my own innate sense of knowing, and that I would have these experiences and more like them again. I have read that it might be useful to have a "symbol diary", somewhere that you can note down different symbols and what they mean to you, so your Guide can communicate clearly. For example, if a rose represents romance to you, then you could draw a rose in your diary with the word "romance" attached to it. Then when your Guide shows you a rose you'll know it means some kind of love affair is on the cards. When writing or drawing your symbols and what they represent, make your intention known to your Guide as you write, and then you will have a shorthand of communication between you. It makes sense I suppose. But I haven't done this. I trust that if my Guide wants me to know something, they'll make it known. I haven't experienced any miscommunication so far.

Another thing that people get caught up on, is giving our Guides names. It's not particularly necessary. Your Guide might offer you a name. For example, my circle leader Gilly Hall told me that one of my Guides was named Johan. When my Native American lady presented herself to me, she didn't offer a name. After I had it confirmed that she was indeed one of my Guides, I thought it only fair to suggest a name for her myself. I proceeded to look up traditional tribal names of the Northern American cultures. I wanted to avoid anything cheesy like Pocahontas or something like that, and I chose "Nanyehi", which is the Cherokee Nation name for Spirit Person. I presented this name to her and she immediately appeared in my mind and offered me a sunflower. I don't think they are particularly fussed about what we call them. It's just something that makes sense to us, since we name each other on the physical plane. Your Guides already know you, and you already know your Guides. Your name or theirs during this embodied experience doesn't matter so much. They use your intuition to communicate. When you consciously reach out and connect with them, you will begin to recognize their voice. You will begin to remember their voice, for this relationship was forged long ago, before you chose to incarnate as your current earthly form.

Meditation Exercise: Effervescent Friends.
Level: Intermediate

One of my teachers, a Medicine Man, gave me this meditation to connect to the Higher Realms. Record it as a self-guided meditation if you are reading this work.

1. Find a comfortable place to sit. It can be beneficial to find a quiet spot in nature for this particular meditation, but it isn't a prerequisite. You can do it at home, hell I've even done it on the London Underground during rush hour. But if you can find a quiet spot in a park, then all the better. Sit with your back straight but comfortable, take a few deep breaths, and close your eyes.

2. Take another deep breath. Hold that breath for two or three seconds, and then let it go. Let your breathing return to normal. I want you to contemplate, acknowledge, and honor that this moment is a sacred moment. Without our parents, we wouldn't be here. Likewise, the same goes for our parents known in some Indigenous traditions as the Cosmic Father, and the Cosmic Mother. Sacred Time is also our father, and Sacred Space is our mother. We are stepping into the present moment of now, and finding the space between our thoughts.

3. With each intake of breath, we breathe in energy. With each out-breath, we transform that energy. We are taking in the process of the collective, the energy of the planet, with every breath, all day long. And we are transmitting ourselves, our own energies, back out to the planet with each exhale. When we sit in meditation, it gives us the time to consciously bring in that which we desire, and to equally send out into the world that which we want to share of ourselves. When we consciously bring in the energy of the world, when we invite it in on the breath,

143

we can intentionally bring in love, joy, vitality, and good intentions. The same goes for when we send our energy back out to the world around us.

4. Now, visualize yourself inside a giant Quartz crystal. Crystals conduct high frequency energy. If there happens to be heavy or negative energy nearby a crystal, it will be instantly transformed by it.

5. Take another deep breath, and pull the energy of your immediate surroundings towards you. The energy is being transformed as it filters through the crystal, and can only enter your own energy field as love, as positivity, and light. Feel that light enter your body and your vibration raise higher.

6. Let your breathing return to normal. Now's the time to invite your Spirit Guides into your Sacred Space, into your Quartz crystal. Remember that you are invoking the power of Highly Evolved Beings. You made a sacred contract with these Light Beings before you came to this planet in your current form. They are old friends. Invite them with reverence, and thank them for any wisdom they may bestow upon you now.

7. Pay attention to your intuition. Has the energy changed around your physical body? Can you feel a presence close by? Equally, take note of any physical sensations. Are there any sensations of cold, or warmth in your hands or other body parts? Do you feel a tingling sensation around your head or your neck? Do you feel nauseous? Take note of these sensations, and then bring your attention back to your breath. Always back to the breath.

8. Now that you are getting used to separating your consciousness from your thoughts, do you recognize anything that doesn't come from you? Faces? An

unfamiliar voice or even a familiar one? Any words or phrases that are suddenly showing up?

9. Even if you don't recognize anything out of the ordinary, be aware that your Spirit Guides are with you now, and downloading your subconscious with helpful information. Thank them for coming close, and tell them that you appreciate the help and knowledge they give to you every day. It's time to end the connection.

10. Your Guides are stepping out of your Sacred Space, and with them, your crystal dissolves into pure light, bathing you and healing you before it disappears completely.

11. Bring your attention back to your breath once again. Begin to notice any sounds around your physical form. Feel the ground or chair beneath you, wiggle your fingers and toes, and slowly, when you're ready, come back to this waking state.

Chapter Twenty-Three: Always Now

The future isn't written. It's an ever-changing tapestry, continually adjusting with the decisions we make in the forever moment of now. There is only now, and everything that has happened, happening, or will happen, is taking place in the constant. So when it comes to Spirit giving us predictions of the future, I have learned that they can observe the possible outcomes from our current actions, and will guide us towards the greater and desired direction where they can. We have made a Soul Agreement, before coming here, and they are well aware of that Soul Agreement since they are the ones we made it with. We are aware of it too but at a superconscious level. Our Soul Agreement is part of our Soul Purpose, the real reason why we are here. It will always pertain to the greater good of the all, and the evolution of our personal spiritual journey. A psychic medium can tune into the Higher Realms, and sense one of the directions a person's life may take, and advise them of a potential outcome. When a person receives this kind of information, they will often either consciously or subconsciously move towards or avert the suggested outcome. If they avoid it, they might then decide that the psychic medium was actually wrong, and that it's all a bunch of mumbo-jumbo. I believe that time doesn't exist in the Spiritual Realms, not in the way that we have it set up here. This is difficult to explain, but since exploring mediumship, I have experienced receiving an answer to something before the question has come up. A good example of this may be what I described in Book One, when one night I sat crying on the beach, begging my Spirit Guides to show themselves. After crying and shouting at the night sky for awhile, I discovered I was sitting next to a chalkboard, mounted on the side of a beach cafe. My name was scrawled on it with the word "hi" over and over again. I believe that my Guides had already anticipated my plight, and taken me to where the answer was before I'd asked the question.

To be mindful of this is to be set free. It really is. It opens up the very real possibility of manifesting that which we desire in our lives. If linear time is an illusion, then we have already done what we want to do, in every conceivable way. We also have the possibility of experiencing what we don't want, since every single outcome is available and waiting in a state of superposition for us to choose it. So we must be mindful of our thoughts. Perception (how we see the world, our beliefs and our personal constructs of reality based on past experiences) breeds potential, thought propagates intention (what we think about is what we focus on) and intention builds creation (our thoughts blend with Universal Consciousness, and together, we create our desired reality).

When we sit in meditation, and connect with our Spirit Guides, we can bring our intended desires into alignment with our Higher Selves. We can manifest that which we desire and let our Guides know what it is we yearn for. Provided these intentions are of benefit to our future and those around us, our Guides will work behind the scenes to help us make our desires a reality. You don't need me to walk you through how to ask your Guides for assistance anymore, we've already been practicing how to do that in the previous chapters. But as promised earlier in this book, we shall further explore connecting with the moment of now in order to recognize that there truly is only the present moment, all the time. The past and the future are memories or possibilities. To manifest the lives we want, and indeed the world we want, we need to be able to tune in and be here now. By tuning in to the present moment, we lay a stable foundation for the choices of the future.

Meditation Exercise: Manifesting in the Forever Now.
Level: Advanced

As always, find yourself a comfortable place to sit where you won't be disturbed. It is best, although not a rule, to attempt this meditation when you are in a peaceful, reflective state of mind. You will get the most beneficial results if there are no mundane matters distracting you such as a recent argument, unpaid financial debt, or work concerns. That being said, connecting with the present moment is always a positive way to put our problems into perspective. But to tap into the now and receive clear, concise insight, it's always best to have a light mind. Record yourself reading the exercise out loud if you are reading the hard copy of this work, and play it back as a guided meditation.

1. Sit with your back straight, but comfortable. Have your feet placed on the ground in front of you, and your hands on the chair rests or on your lap. Before we begin, suck in a couple of deep breaths, and on the exhale, dispel all negative thoughts and energy out with the breath. Feel free to clap your hands in a circle around your torso, clearing the energy. Alternatively, flick the air away from you with your hands in an outward motion, around your head and body. Feel the energy clear around you. Return your hands back to their resting position, and close your eyes.

2. Let your breathing return to normal. Feel your feet connecting with the ground and your legs growing heavy. Let your arms relax and go heavy, and feel your shoulders gently drop. Let your jaw unclench and soften. Imagine the air you are breathing in as a luminous white cloud, floating just in front of you. Pull it in and let it fill you with white light, reaching all corners of your mind and even down to your fingertips and toes. Continue to

do this until the white light has reached every inch of your physical being.

3. Now imagine pulling up the Earth's healing energy through your feet, grounding you in the here and now. Imagine the energy as a glowing green light, and feel it rise up through your calves, your thighs, around the Root Chakra, up past the Sacral Chakra, the Solar Plexus Chakra, and as it reaches the heart, feel your Heart Chakra unwind and expand in front of you, sending out the healing Earth energy to the world and blending with the ever-abundant luminous cloud of white light that you continue to breathe in. Feel the glowing green light continue up past your Throat Chakra, and out through the top of your head to the Higher Realms above. You are now held in the here and now between the Earth and the Spirit World, in perfect unison with both.

4. Imagine now, a golden spiral staircase appearing just above you. It winds upwards and into the sky, and as you raise your light from your body, go towards it and begin walking up.

5. As you ascend the spiral staircase, it slowly and gently begins to move in the opposite direction. It doesn't cause you to lose balance or experience any discomfort. You are walking upwards and making progress, but at the same time the staircase winds down, and you realize that you are in the constant moment of now, as that is all there is.

6. You begin to notice life events from your past taking place in the blue skies around you. You see familiar faces, family members, friends, you can see places and random events from your younger years. You may also see events that you don't recall witnessing, and you may see faces of friends who you don't recognize. These are other life events, and these are people you have known in other

lifetimes. They may be from past lives or from future ones. The actions you are taking in this current lifetime, determine what those future lives will be.

7. As you continue to walk up the staircase, walking in the same spot, these lives unfold around you. Float away from the staircase now and back to your physical body. We are not done yet. We are now truly anchored in the present moment.

8. Continue to breathe in the glowing white light, and drawing the energy up from the Earth. Bring your attention to your Third Eye Chakra, at your forehead. Feel it uncurl and expand in front of you. An indigo light shines forth from it, quickening your Highest Self and intuitive vision. You shall connect now, with your Guides. Ask them to come close, invite them into your Sacred Space and feel their presence rising near you. Remember that these are Highly Evolved Beings. They comprehend worlds we can currently only imagine. They know you and they have known you in other lifetimes. This friendship is a sacred bond. Be mindful of that now while you begin to concentrate on the greatest, most wonderful vision of your future that you can imagine. You may have even seen it while you walked the staircase before.

9. Bring your attention to your Throat Chakra, feel it opening wide before you and expanding as the color blue. This will give you the ability to clearly articulate that which you want to manifest as your reality. You don't need to physically speak. Just set your intention to link with your Spirit Guides while you concentrate on the greatest version of your future and what you desire. There is only the moment of now. Every possibility is waiting for you to choose it. Choose wisely, choose well, and above all else, choose with love.

10. Notice any changes in the atmosphere around your physical body. Take note of any ideas or thoughts that present themselves to you now. Your team of Guides are advising you and you are receiving their insights whether you are conscious of them or not. Trust that the greater good is being downloaded to your subconscious via the superconscious. Your soul will know what to do with this information.

11. Thank your Spirit Guides for this joint manifestation. Thank them for their wisdom and for always being there. You can begin to close down the connection now. Draw the glowing green energy back down from the top of your head, and close the Crown Chakra as you go. Feel the energy move down past your Third Eye Chakra. Pull back the brilliant blue stream of light shooting from it, and close it before moving down to your Throat Chakra. Again, pull back the energy, and see it close like a bud. As the light moves down to your chest and past your Heart Chakra, close it as you go. When we close our Heart Chakra we prevent letting in any negative energy from external influences around us. It will open again naturally and when needed through your day-to-day life. Bring the light down through your Solar Plexus Chakra, closing it as you go, your Sacral Chakra, closing it as you go, and your Root Chakra, which will remain open, to keep you grounded. Bring the light back down your legs and into the Earth. Continue to breathe in the glowing white light in front of you, and begin to notice any sounds around your physical body.

12. Feel the chair beneath you, wiggle your fingers and toes, take a few deep breaths, and when you feel ready, open your eyes. You are here, you are now, and you are alive. There is only now. All the time.

Chapter Twenty-Four: The Soldier

I finished writing *Letting Glow* on the anniversary of my mother's passing. I knew that would be the day that I would finish it. I'd known it for months, since my Guides gave me the information when I began to write. I wandered into Barnes Healing Church in London two nights later. It was a cold winter's evening. I'd been there before, and nearly every time I'd received a message from the demonstrating medium, and almost every time those mediums told me I had a strong connection with Spirit. I went there on this night hoping to hear something from my mom. The first Christmas without her had been tough, really tough, and I'd spent the anniversary of her death drinking myself into a stupor up on Hampstead Heath while watching the winter sunset. I arrived at the church two nights later with no expectations, only a quiet hope, and placed myself somewhere in the middle of the small congregation, on the left-hand side.

Every Sunday, there would be a demonstration of mediumship from a visiting medium. No money exchanged hands, no prior information was given to the medium by the attendees. A new medium would visit each week and attempt to reassure and prove to the audience that their departed loved ones still existed in Spirit. I'd witnessed this enough times to be convinced it was one hundred percent real. The evidence given was usually spot on. I'd received evidence myself, from my mom, three months after she had passed. It was undoubtedly from my mom, through a lady named Janet Neville. She told me things that night that no one else knew, and also brought through a friend who had passed when we were young. It had helped me immensely.

Some mediums that I'd seen in action were better than others. Each worked in their own unique way. I don't remember the lady's name, who stood up on the platform that night and gave the service, but I do remember her eyes locking with mine before she told me that someone was there for me. I'll remember it for the rest of my life.

"I have a gentleman here," she told me. "A family member. He's wearing a blue suit, and standing very upright. As though he were once in the military."

I don't know much about my family history. My mother's mom had died before I was born, and her father a few days after, and as I've mentioned already, my father was adopted. I hadn't seen him since I was eighteen years old, some twenty-seven years before, and we'd never talked about his adoption when I was young.

"He has thinning dark hair," she went on. "Actually, more than thinning," she smiled. "Does that sound like anyone you know?"

Mediums don't like long-winded answers. A simple yes or no will suffice. Too much information, and they run the risk of being led and accused of guesswork.

"It might do," I offered unhelpfully. "I don't really know my family tree very well."

The dark hair and blue suit kind of sounded like my dad, I thought. Despite his abhorrent and unforgivable treatment of my mom, I remember him as a charismatic man considered to be the life and soul of the party, as they said in those days. He was handsome, he was charming. He had a multitude of demons from his upbringing and serving in overseas territories with the British Army. He had been a decorated soldier, and my mom had told me the story of how her own father had to buy him out of the military when she was pregnant. He was overseas someplace and no one could reach him. When I was a kid, he had a major operation to remove one of his lungs. I have no idea why, there's no one left to tell me. And last time I saw him he still smoked a pack of cigarettes a day and enjoyed a drink. If those two things didn't get him then surely the recent COVID pandemic would have. I'd tried to track him down from time to time; we'd lost touch completely after I moved away. I tried once again when I returned to England after twenty years. I couldn't even find my stepbrothers on any social media platforms. He was a ghost, and well, if this woman was about to give me evidence that it was him who had come through, I guess he was an actual ghost now.

"He was adopted," she said, catching me completely by surprise. I had to remember to breathe.

Alright. Well I suppose the debate was settled.

"He's full of regret," she went on. "Regret for not being there when you needed him. He's saying that your current work is very different from what his was. Your lifestyle is different to his."

This was true. I'd been working sporadically as an actor and I have a relatively, albeit financially challenged, relaxed lifestyle. He had been the boss of a large steelworks factory in middle England. When he wasn't at work he was working at home on paperwork for work.

"He's telling me now that he regrets how he treated you and your mother," she went on. "I think I have your father with me."

"I think you do too," I replied.

"He says that you chose him and your mother to be your parents before you were born. He didn't know then that you are an old soul. Older than him, he says, at soul level. He's saying now that you are a highly evolved spiritual being and he talks of you with reverence. He's saying that you are about to go on to great things."

She paused.

"Well this is interesting," she said, cocking her head to one side. She stood for a long moment in silence.

"My Guides are stepping in," she added eventually, and then went quiet again.

"They rarely interrupt," she said after a few more moments, frowning. Then she fixed her gaze on me again, a quizzical expression on her face. "They're telling me that *you* are connected to Spirit, is that true?"

"Well," I replied. "People keep telling me that I am..." I trailed off.

"Are you a medium also?" she asked.

"I'm in a development circle," I told her. "I've only just started. I'm not planning to be a medium. But people keep telling me that I will be."

"Wow," she said, looking at me with an undisguised expression of awe that made me feel very self-conscious. "They're telling me that you have a very powerful connection to Spirit. They're saying that your calling is to pass information from the Spirit World to this one and that you've written a book on the subject."

"I mean, yeah I just finished one," I mumbled. "The other day actually. I don't know what I'm going to do with it though."

"Well they're saying that you can do anything you want. They're saying that whatever path you choose to focus on, whether it be mediumship, healing, trance mediumship, or transcription, that it will open one door after another," she continued giving me that same look and nodding while smiling. I became aware of the other people in the church turning to look at me. The small audience was usually made up of older people. Grey haircuts and thinning crowns began to spiral in my direction. I have to admit, for a couple of seconds, my ego kicked in and I felt like a wild, young spiritual rockstar.

"Your dad says he is sorry," she went on. "He says that mental illness wasn't routinely recognized in those days, and that he wishes he would have been able to get the help that is available today."

Wow. I felt tears begin to rise. I was having a conversation with my dad for the first time in twenty-seven years. It also broke my heart a little.

"He sends you his love," she said, wrapping things up. "And I will send him yours."

Chapter Twenty-Five: Maureen

I'm no expert on grief. I haven't received any counselling, I haven't joined any support groups. As of writing, it is nearing the two-year mark of my mother's passing from this world into the next.

It is near impossible to describe the experience. What I am going through might be very different to what you have been through or will go through. There are many factors to consider, including the relationship you had with your loved one. Were they a family member or friend? Were you close or estranged? Were they young when they passed or older? Were there any unresolved issues or things you wished you would have said? Are you someone who is in touch with your emotions or do you prefer to stifle them? One thing I have learned over this past year and a half, is that our relationship with our loved one goes on. Even the most skeptical person can acknowledge this as truth, even someone who steadfastly believes that there is no afterlife could agree that you need to continue working on your relationship with the deceased, if only for your own peace of mind, even if you believe that relationship to be one-sided since their passing. Most of us wish we had said more. Most of us wish we could have given more. Through the experiences I've so far had since my mom passed to the other side, I've come to the conclusion that we still can.

Our loved ones are still with us. But even though I believe that to be an absolute truth, it doesn't stop me from hurting. It doesn't take away my regret. It makes it ever so slightly easier, but I would still give away years of my own life to have one more day with my mom here.

The first months were the hardest. I would cry a lot. It was the most gut-wrenching, raw emotion I've ever experienced.

I've lost friends before, I've had romantic relationships end where I wrongly believed I couldn't live without that person in my life. But to lose a parent, when they've always been there since day one, is its own kind of hurt. I can't imagine the pain of losing a child or a spouse, I only hope that through sharing my own experience, it might help you with yours.

Something that has gradually built over these months, is how my mother's life has expanded beyond how I'd previously witnessed it. I no longer selfishly see my mom's life exclusively through mine. In death, her life has become an eternal loop where age no longer touches her. Her hopes and dreams and aspirations from when she was young now appear current and vital despite me having seen her age, or that she is no longer physically here. The person I had become used to as she grew old has become young again. I had, of course, talked with my mother about her life previous to her giving birth to me. She'd told me stories of her younger years and her own upbringing. But it quickly became even bigger than that. Why had I never asked her deeper questions? What had she secretly dreamt of accomplishing when she was young? How did she feel as someone in her seventies compared to who she was when she was thirty or forty? What did she regret? Who had she loved? Did she believe in life after death? I am deeply regretful that these things had fallen by the wayside with complacency and the familiarity between us. I feel like I missed a massive opportunity to know the woman who was closer to me than anyone else in the world. How could that have happened?

I wish we'd talked about these things. And then I wish we'd talked about them again. And again. Until I could recall every single detail of it all at will. Until I'd listened to every hope and dream she ever had from every possible angle, until I could remember every single story and name and date and place.

Record your loved ones talking. Take pictures. Put those pictures on hard drives and take more pictures. Ask questions. Ask *every* question. What books changed their lives? What songs? What movies? Why? Who was their secret crush when they were a kid? What happened to that person? What does their home town mean to them? What do they wish they'd always done? Can they still do it? Do they have any rituals they do each day? What annoys them more than anything? Where do they wish they would have always travelled to? Take them there if it's possible. If you haven't asked these questions, and are still able to, I implore you to ask them now. Our loved ones are still with us when they pass, and they still communicate with us. But as we're beginning to learn, they come through in symbols, images, and feelings. Occasionally we might be lucky enough to actually hear or even see them, but for the most part, we won't be able to get the details we could while they were still on the physical plane.

I wish that I'd been around more for her as she grew older. I wish I'd have had those more poignant conversations with her and recorded them. And then had them all over and recorded them again. And this wouldn't just be for me. It would be in honor of what was once a vibrant life that had quietly grown dimmer and slipped away without anyone noticing. She deserved more than that. We all do.

I'm once again sitting here in her house, as I oftentimes did while writing *Letting Glow*. I alternate between here and London every couple of weeks. I'm sitting in her spot in the living room. I haven't moved anything. I keep the place clean and visit as often as I can. But with each visit it becomes more apparent that it's not sustainable. Mostly for financial reasons, but as time goes on, emotional ones as well. I've kept the place untouched for almost two years now, and while it probably helped with the initial stages of grief, I wonder if it's now doing me a disservice, and preventing me from moving forward. I'm going to miss it. The smell is still the same as it's always been. Everywhere I look there are ornaments, pictures, and furniture placed exactly where my mom placed them. And I worry that the further I move forward in life when I soon say goodbye to it, the harder these things will become to recall. I guess that's inevitable, and I guess that's the way life is supposed to be. If money wasn't an issue, I'd probably keep it exactly as it is for my entire life. But I know that wouldn't really do me any good. It's somehow comforting to be here, I grew up here, but ultimately it just makes me miss her more, and keeps grief very close to me.

One of the hardest things for me to accept and own, is how I behaved towards my mom from time to time. I found a video file on my laptop of us both hanging out at my apartment in London. At first I was pleased, I'd completely missed it when going through all of the photos. But then I watched it, and I was deeply ashamed. I was recording it for a family friend, showing them the new apartment, while my mom sat talking nearby. I was being impatient with her, for no reason other than I could sometimes be a selfish idiot, and I was ignoring everything she was saying as I walked around the flat. Towards the end of the video she asks me to come and sit beside her, so that we could send a joint message to the family friend I was recording it for. I didn't even want to do that, and dismissed the request as silly and ended the video. It's not the worst thing in the world, but it's a horrible reminder of how I sometimes talked to her: reverting back to my teenage self and thinking I knew better. I've never watched it again. And I won't delete it because she's on it.

Alright, the tears are coming again now.

I have to remind myself that we had many good times, many adventures, when we were two best friends. We went to concerts together, the movies, we travelled to other countries, we'd go shopping and go out for coffee. There were many laughs, and she knows that I love her. I tell her every day, as I did before she passed.

My mom (or my mum, as I would usually pronounce it) was a lovely lady that just wanted to be loved, after a lifetime of people taking advantage of her from a young age. And she still is, in Spirit, she's still that lovely lady she always was. She has come through for me multiple times with different mediums. The specifics have been so on point that I can't doubt them. She has come through as wise when I needed her to be wise, she has come through as playful and sometimes practical, and she has come through as loving. She has come through without other mediums and I've received strong impressions from her directly in answer to my questions. I even heard her once, right beside me, earlier this year.

The week that I submitted *Letting Glow* to a few publishers, and just after my experience with my dad in Barnes Healing Church, Laura and I received an incredible offer to go to the Caribbean for a holiday, completely free of charge. It came about through Laura's workplace, and a generous suggestion from her boss. I don't believe that it was coincidental that I finished my first book about living in the moment, manifestation, and Spirit, the same week that the offer appeared. It was also the first anniversary of my mom passing away, and the place we were going to visit was one of the last places I ever went on holiday with my mom. So we suddenly found ourselves on a beach in Antigua, when I had perhaps £50 in my bank account and multiple debts after the pandemic, little work, and of course all of the expenses that come with losing a loved one. I shouldn't have been able to go there, and needless to say, thanks to Laura, we had a wonderful and much-needed break after what had been the roughest year of our lives.

When it came time to check in for our return flight to England, we picked the best spot we could find on the plane. Two seats on their own by the emergency exit, with plenty of legroom. When we boarded the plane we discovered we'd been moved to the center row of four seats with people in front and behind us. I tried to get our original seats back but the flight attendants weren't interested, and I was mumbling my complaints as we shuffled over and began stuffing our bags into the overhead compartments and our books and snacks under the seats in front of us. When the flight began to taxi along the runway, and no one else sat beside us and we had the entire row of four seats to ourselves, I heard my mother's voice, as clear as a bell. I wasn't thinking of her at the time, I was just counting our blessings when I realized no one was coming to sit beside us.

"Well where was I going to sit?" I heard my mom laugh.

Chapter Twenty-Six: The Waltz

This reality is not the totality of infinity. There is more. Beyond the stars, beyond time, beyond thought and beyond emotion. The way we've been taught and the direction the human race has taken is off kilter with the planet. That's a given. Everybody knows that now. We are out of synch with our environment and we are out of synch with ourselves and each other. Most people are out of synch with Spirit. This version of reality that everyone's doing doesn't work anymore. Take a look around and see for yourself. Most of the systems we have in place that are supposed to create a better life for us fail to do what they were put in place to do. Our political systems continue to promote nothing but disagreement and disarrangement, and elevate narcissists to positions of power. Our healthcare systems are in constant turmoil and underfunded, and produce year-long waiting lists for public access to modern medicine and health services. Our economical setup produces poverty at an ever-increasing rate, along with inequality and divisions in social class structures, which in turn results in heinous injustices and disparity. The planet is being plundered for its natural resources to increase imaginary numbers in an imaginary economy that we've all decided to accept as real. The rich get richer, and it'll stay that way until the world demands total transparency of incomes. We look to our phones that we invented for answers from celebrities about how we should present ourselves and act and what tribe we belong to and even how we should save the planet. We are turning to billionaires to tell us how to save the planet. Think about that for a second. Those who have accumulated the top 1% of material wealth in the world are telling us what we must do to end poverty and save the environment. 1.2 billion people on the planet don't have electricity. 2 billion don't have access to clean water. We value material wealth and use it as a measure of success and we seek it out, but for the most part we don't want to work for it because in our core we know it's not actually of real value at all. If during your last minutes of this life you peacefully slip into the night congratulating yourself on how much money you accumulated then you will have squandered your time here. And you will know this.

Love is not an emotion. It's a force. A force like gravity. And it is in all things and the answer to every question. Literally the answer to every question. If the answer comes from love, then it is the way. If it isn't, if you don't recognize the answer to your predicament as coming from the force that is love, then it is coming from something that doesn't serve you, or the greater good. Love is a force of conscience. Love is a direct link to your Higher Self. Would your Higher Self do what you are about to do? If the answer is no, then don't do it. It's really that simple. Before you start the argument. Before you yell at the guy who just cut you off in traffic. Before you uncork the bottle of whiskey – because this includes self-love too. If everyone would collectively practice this then the problems we face today in the world would begin to dissolve. But to be able to answer life's daily questions from the stance of love takes practice. It takes learning to step back from the thoughts. Learning to step forward beyond the thoughts, learning to sidestep around the distractions. Learning to navigate anger. Learning to not let negative opinions trigger or bother you. When you can get to that place where you can dance, then you know you are playing the game correctly. The answer is always there. In the silence. *Between the thoughts.* Every time. And life will begin to flow. You need to learn to dance between the ifs and the buts and the what-abouts, since they are just habitual thinking. The answer is with your highest self first.

And I know it's not our fault. We showed up and everything was already like this. We didn't start the fire. And money can bring joy and nourishment and excitement and opportunity. But only because it was set up like that. You can get to where you need to be without the hustle. Without the struggle. Go with love. Go with the intuitive knowing that instantly arises in answer to your question. Before the over questioning thoughts barge in. Go with your heart. Go with trust that things are as they should be whether the current circumstances are perceived rightly or wrongly, because we have generated the current outcome in the first place. If you perceive your life situation as dire, then worry and doubt and fear will only prolong it. Dance around worry and doubt and fear. Let the band clash and bang and keep on playing in the background. Don't click on the pop-up window. Go to "settings" and don't allow notifications from trivial things. Let them be. Attach no significance to them. You know your higher truth already. Because you've taken the time to sit in the silence. Because you continually practice stepping back from your thoughts and simply observe them. You are not your thoughts. You are the one watching them. With regular practice, you will glide between them, and you will waltz around them.

Chapter Twenty-Seven: In Closing

I understand that everything written here can be a lot to take in. I understand that even though you may want to believe the things that are written here, doubt might prevent you from doing so. I get it, because I've been there, repeatedly. I wouldn't have believed everything written in these books three years ago. A Creator? That seemed plausible. Something of higher intelligence that set life into motion? Why not. But ghosts and stuff? I mean, I'd had a few brief experiences here and there, but they were always fleeting. And people seemed to think there were more important things in life to concentrate on. Things like deciding what to do with your life and earning a living.

I remember, in my twenties, being acutely aware of being in my twenties. I was totally in tune with my youth. I had zero interest in working for a living. I did it, but only out of necessity. I wasn't lazy, I didn't shy away from it. I just couldn't get excited about making money for someone else's dreams and lifestyle. It seemed kind of pointless. And I'd never found that thing that I wanted to do. While friends were off learning to become carpenters, teachers, soldiers, accountants and hairdressers, all I wanted to do was to live. To really live. To feel emotions, to love and travel and experience things. But there came the problem of having to make money. I knew that it shouldn't be set up the way it was. It didn't seem to align with the bonfire burning in my soul. How could the two things be polar opposites? To live free, I needed to slave away at a crappy job that I had no interest in. I would find work that would sustain me for awhile, and I'd make enough money to be able to move on. I travelled the world, I went on adventures, I loved, I had my heart broken, became arrogant, had my ego smashed to pieces, went nuts for awhile, drank too much, partied, and somehow, found my way back home again. To square one. To England, where I'd started. My mom was still here and things were how they were again. I'd also found a loving, amazing life partner along the way, and we started over. London. Day one, at forty-two years old.

Then the world changed. People got sick. Summers got hotter and winters got colder. Wars were declared. The financial cost of living became increasingly expensive. My mom left this Earth. I personally felt like I'd just been getting started, and then the rug was pulled out from underneath all of us.

In many ancient nations, I would be considered an elder by now. I don't feel like an elder. Not physically. But spiritually? I guess I kind of do. I guess I always have. I only just thought of that, to be honest. People would rarely want to talk with me about the metaphysical. I'd bring it up, for years and years, through my twenties, through my thirties. Most of the time my friends wouldn't care to indulge me. And when someone did, we'd always hit a brick wall. What's out there? No one really knows. Except now I believe that I'm beginning to learn. It's happening fast, and I'm sharing it as fast as I can with the world. As I learn it, I say it. Or I write it. Whether people believe me or not is a different story, and that's not my concern. Some people are going to think I'm nuts. Some friends already tease me. "Ask your Spirit Guides what to do," they'll say. I get it. It's fine. Everyone has to find their own way. If these books can help a little, then great.

I shall continue to write. The more I learn the more I'll share. I guess it was meant to be this all along. I guess not finding a conventional job, and travelling through life at a deeper level was my work experience. I just wish it hadn't taken losing the person I loved most in the world to make this my work.

I've witnessed some amazing things while I've been writing these books over the last two years. Things that have proven to me beyond a shadow of a doubt that the mystical isn't that mystical after all. It's real. We just need to focus to find it. Even if you are struggling to believe all that's been written here, I encourage you to take on the exercises and practice. See what happens. Be open to it. And hey, let me know how you get on. I'm easily reachable on social media. I genuinely want to know.

To finish this book, I asked some of my teachers (three of the best mediums and spiritual teachers in the world) what advice they would give to anyone aspiring to strengthen their connection with Spirit, and who possibly wanted to go into mediumship. I asked James Van Praagh his advice on how to push through moments of doubt, or when things don't seem to be working. Had he ever experienced these things when he was starting his journey of mediumship?

"Don't get caught up in the complexity of the simplicity," he told me. "You are just the observer, the voice box. You can't control it. Every connection is a lesson. It's always different and sometimes it doesn't always work."

"But what carried you through the hard parts?" I asked him. "When you were developing as a medium, what helped you keep going forward?"

"The Bodhi Tree always helped me," he replied, referring to a spiritual bookshop that used to be in Los Angeles. "The wow part. The excitement carried me through, the enthusiasm. The learning process itself."

I asked Gordon Smith, hailed as Britain's most accurate medium, the same questions.

"Life can sometimes get in the way and block you," Gordon told me. "Find the quiet, and take your time. There's no rush. And when you do start making a connection, because you will with practice, just go with it and let it come. If you're reading for someone, keep talking with them. Say what you see. If you get an apple, don't make it an orchard. Surrender to it and don't try. Open up layer by layer."

Claire Broad is a medium and author; she was my first teacher and has now become a good friend. Her book *What the Dead are Dying to Teach Us* helped get me through the initial months after my mom passed.

"I've learned that I am the only obstacle between myself and the Spirit World," she told me. "For me, the process of developing a strong connection was as much about learning to trust myself, as it was about trusting the information that the Spirit World gave me. When I stepped out of my own way, Spirit stepped in. Work on letting go of expectations and over time, with dedication, the rest will follow."

"How did you deal with friends and family that had a hard time understanding your venture into mediumship?" I asked her.

"If family and friends can't accept your truth, that's OK. Love is not about control. Love is not about need. Love is not about expectations. Give those you love the freedom to be themselves, whilst also setting yourself free from the need for their approval or acceptance. Walk your path with conviction. Those who resonate with you, will find you."

Chapter Twenty-Eight: The Day After

Do you remember how, at the start of this book, I wrote that I was being guided to finish writing on August 31st? Well yesterday, August 30th, I finished the previous chapter and thought that I was done. I was happy with it, and a day early was close enough. I could have stretched the truth and signed off with August 31st, but I don't want to cheat anyone or make stuff up. All that's been written here about my own personal experiences is 100% true. I believed I had nothing more to say until I eventually write Book Three of this series. I will, of course, have to go through this entire text a couple of times before I submit it to my publisher. I'll have to check spelling, rearrange a sentence here or there (I could do that forever, you have to force yourself to draw a line somewhere), but other than checking details, I considered the book finished.

Then I woke up early this morning with a very familiar feeling. As I drifted in the Theta state, before my thoughts crept in, I was instantly aware that I was mid-download. *They* were giving me some very profound information.

"Do you still want this?" That's what they'd asked last time, all those years ago, when I felt this happening before. I'd panicked then, and snapped myself wide awake, watching as a glowing grid dissolved before my eyes and the connection was instantly broken. I didn't do that this morning. I lay very still, acknowledged that I was receiving something special, and did my damnedest to concentrate on every last detail.

What follows is quite radical, and might be difficult to comprehend. It's going to be difficult to write. But as I received the information, I was also being given the experience of it, and it was the simplest thing in the world. It made perfect sense, and I'll try and do my best to convey it as smoothly as I can here. I considered saving it until Book Three. It's way heavier than the things we have talked about so far. But then I realized it actually aligns perfectly with what has already been written. In fact, it completes some of what's in the mid-section of this book, and I don't think I would be able to grasp what I'm about to relay here if I hadn't already researched and wrote the information in the chapter "Manifesting In The Multiverse Of Madness". Added to that, I received this message today, the day when my Guides told me I would finish this book, all the way back in March. So obviously, they intend for it to be included here.

We are multidimensional beings. As we choose from an endless array of possibilities that exist in superposition waiting for us to pick a direction, so does the universe align with our intended outcome, and gives us the reality we want. No matter if we've chosen that reality at a conscious, subconscious, or superconscious level. Our futures exist across an endless horizon of options, with each scenario evolving, developing, and being molded and played out dependent on our current choices. Remember, you are constantly creating your own universe, *manifesting* your life into existence, and so is every other version of you out there in the multiverse. Each decision that you make here and now brings about a new outcome in every reality, meaning the potential outcome of every decision is already there, suspended in a state of superposition in the constant moment of now, waiting for you to choose it, *whether you choose it or not.*

Are you still with me? Alright good, because here comes the big one.

I'm going to use myself as an example, to try and keep the language as simple as possible within this abstract retelling of the information I received. Our greatest obstacle when trying to explain the mystical is our language. So here we go.

If there are multiple universes upon universes of possibility, where I've chosen in this forever moment of now to do every conceivable thing I could possibly do (in ultimate reality everything that has happened, is happening, or ever will happen is taking place right now), then it stands to reason that if this theory is correct, I've already died in many, many of those realities. Right now, out there in the multiverse, I'm already dead. For some reason, I'm consciously choosing to experience this physical reality, but out there, there is a reality where I'm experiencing what comes after. An ultimate reality. And if all we have is the current moment of now, then I'm already dead.

The direct experience that I had upon waking this morning, was sitting and talking with my mother, and a good friend of mine who is currently still alive. Except in the experience I was having, we were already passed over. All three of us. I was being told that just like how we choose to manifest our desired reality in this life, the same principle applies when we pass over to the other side. Except over there, we have the infinite at our fingertips. Whatever we choose, manifests instantaneously. We don't have to work for it. We don't have to go through a physical process of constructing it. We choose it, and it happens. Therefore, my mom is out there choosing to experience a reality where I'm already with her. She's well aware of this one that I'm in right now, this physical reality where I'm writing these words, just as she's aware that she was also recently part of it. But time works differently there, and what I briefly experienced this morning was her choosing a future reality with me, since I'm already there, right now. The friend who's still currently alive in this world was there to demonstrate that further. Neale Donald Walsch touched on this in his book *Home with God*. He stated that when we pass over, we can choose who greets us when we get there, even if that person is still alive.

We are multi, multi, multifarious beings ad infinitum, existing on all planes of every reality simultaneously. That's why when we think of our loved ones in Spirit, they are with us in an instant. Time doesn't exist in ultimate reality, and our loved ones are now part of that ultimate reality, and we are part of that ultimate reality too. Right now. We are there with them, even while our primary focus is on this dense embodied experience. Thus they are here with us right now also. It's mind-bending to us in this realm. Yet in the ultimate realms it's incredibly simple, and everything we choose is just a conscious thought away. Everything we choose is achieved through intuition. Thought breeds creation both here and on the other side. But there it is possible to co-achieve with one another on multiple levels of awareness at exactly the same time, since we understand that we are all connected, everything is happening right now, and there is only One. We co-create in our current embodied life, but in the hereafter, all levels of existence can be blended into one experience. And that's happening there right now alongside this reality.

When a medium tunes in to the Higher Realms, they are actively blending the supraconscious with the conscious. They are aligning what is mystical to us with the non-mystical. They pass on information to us from our loved ones in Spirit, and we implement that information into our physical reality.

So there we have it. I told you we were going to go deep. I also promised that we'd both know more about the Spirit World now, than we did at the start of this book. I hope that I have delivered on those promises.

Always remember that intention is everything. Our loved ones walk with us and are whispering in our ear. We just need to quieten our minds and listen. Thank you for joining me on this journey. Raise your vibration, and glow.

Phill Webster, Richmond upon Thames, August 31st, 2022. 14.29 pm.

O-BOOKS

SPIRITUALITY

O is a symbol of the world, of oneness and unity; this eye
represents knowledge and insight. We publish titles on general
spirituality and living a spiritual life. We aim to inform and
help you on your own journey in this life.
If you have enjoyed this book, why not tell other readers
by posting a review on your preferred book site?

Recent bestsellers from O-Books are:

Heart of Tantric Sex
Diana Richardson
Revealing Eastern secrets of deep love and intimacy
to Western couples.
Paperback: 978-1-90381-637-0 ebook: 978-1-84694-637-0

Crystal Prescriptions
The A-Z guide to over 1,200 symptoms and their healing crystals
Judy Hall
The first in the popular series of eight books, this handy little
guide is packed as tight as a pill bottle with crystal remedies
for ailments.
Paperback: 978-1-90504-740-6 ebook: 978-1-84694-629-5

Shine On
David Ditchfield and J S Jones
What if the aftereffects of a near-death experience were undeniable? What if a person could suddenly produce high-quality paintings of the afterlife, or if they acquired the ability to compose classical symphonies?
Meet: David Ditchfield.
Paperback: 978-1-78904-365-5 ebook: 978-1-78904-366-2

The Way of Reiki
The Inner Teachings of Mikao Usui
Frans Stiene
The roadmap for deepening your understanding of the system of Reiki and rediscovering your
True Self.
Paperback: 978-1-78535-665-0 ebook: 978-1-78535-744-2

You Are Not Your Thoughts.
Frances Trussell
The journey to a mindful way of being, for those who want to truly know the power of mindfulness.
Paperback: 978-1-78535-816-6 ebook: 978-1-78535-817-3

The Mysteries of the Twelfth Astrological House
Fallen Angels
Carmen Turner-Schott, MSW, LISW
Everyone wants to know more about the most misunderstood house in astrology — the twelfth astrological house.
Paperback: 978-1-78099-343-0 ebook: 978-1-78099-344-7

WhatsApps from Heaven
Louise Hamlin
An account of a bereavement and the extraordinary
signs — including WhatsApps — that a retired
law lecturer received from her deceased husband.
Paperback: 978-1-78904-947-3 ebook: 978-1-78904-948-0

The Holistic Guide to Your Health
& Wellbeing Today
Oliver Rolfe
A holistic guide to improving your complete health,
both inside and out.
Paperback: 978-1-78535-392-5 ebook: 978-1-78535-393-2

Cool Sex
Diana Richardson and Wendy Doeleman
For deeply satisfying sex, the real secret is to reduce the heat,
to cool down. Discover the empowerment and fulfilment
of sex with loving mindfulness.
Paperback: 978-1-78904-351-8 ebook: 978-1-78904-352-5

Creating Real Happiness A to Z
Stephani Grace
Creating Real Happiness A to Z will help you understand
the truth that you are not your ego
(conditioned self).
Paperback: 978-1-78904-951-0 ebook: 978-1-78904-952-7

A Colourful Dose of Optimism

Jules Standish

It's time for us to look on the bright side, by boosting
our mood and lifting our spirit, both in our interiors,
as well as in our closet.

Paperback: 978-1-78904-927-5 ebook: 978-1-78904-928-2

Readers of ebooks can buy or view any of these bestsellers by
clicking on the live link in the title. Most titles are published
in paperback and as an ebook. Paperbacks are available in
traditional bookshops. Both print and ebook formats are
available online.

Find more titles and sign up to our readers' newsletter at
www.o-books.com

Follow O books on Facebook at **O-books**

For video content, author interviews and more, please subscribe to our YouTube channel:

O-BOOKS Presents

Follow us on social media for book news, promotions and more:

Facebook: O-Books

Instagram: @o_books_mbs

Twitter: @obooks

Tik Tok: @ObooksMBS

www.o-books.com